Better Homes and Gardens®

BREAD MACHINE BOUNTY

BETTER HOMES AND GARDENS® BOOKS
Des Moines

P9-EMQ-236

BREAD MACHINE BOUNTY
Editor: Jennifer Darling
Contributing Editor: Jennifer Speer Ramundt
Graphic Designer: Ernest Shelton
Production Editor: Paula Forest
Test Kitchen Product Supervisor: Marilyn Cornelius
Food Stylist: Jennifer Peterson
Cover Photographer: Perry Struse

BETTER HOMES AND GARDENS® BOOKS
An Imprint of Meredith® Books
President, Book Group: Joseph J. Ward
Vice President and Editorial Director: Elizabeth P. Rice
Executive Editor: Connie Schrader
Art Director: Ernest Shelton
Prepress Production Manager: Randall Yontz
Test Kitchen Director: Sharon Stilwell

On the cover:
Almond Loaf (page 128)
Apricot-Almond Wreath (page 136)
Bran-Bulgur Butterhorns (page 116)
Cracked Wheat Italian Bread (page 108)
Cranberry-Nut Sourdough Bread (page 73)
Dried Tomato and Pine Nut Bread (page 48)
Egg Bread (page 87)
Golden Onion Bread (page 110)
Granary Bread (page 32)
Sour Cream-Wheat Dinner Rolls (page 114)

WE CARE!

All of us at Better Homes and Gardens® Books are dedicated to providing you with the information and ideas you need to create tasty foods. We welcome your comments and suggestions. Write us at: Better Homes and Gardens® Books, Cookbook Editorial Department, RW-240, 1716 Locust Street, Des Moines, IA 50309-3023

If you would like to order additional copies of any of our books, call 1-800-678-2803 or check with your local bookstore.

Our seal assures you that every recipe in *Bread Machine Bounty* has been tested in the Better Homes and Gardens® Test Kitchen. This means that each recipe is practical and reliable, and meets our high standards of taste appeal. We guarantee your satisfaction with this book for as long as you own it.

©Copyright 1992 by Meredith Corporation, Des Moines, Iowa.
All Rights Reserved. Printed in the United States of America.
First Edition. Printing Number and Year: 10 9   99 98 97 96
Library of Congress Catalog Card Number: 92-82901
ISBN: 0-696-01992-2

CONTENTS

Bread Basics

5

White Breads

16

Wheat Breads

27

Sourdough Breads

64

Rye Breads

75

Egg Breads

86

Shaped Breads, Rolls, and Coffee Cakes

101

INTRODUCTION

Nothing welcomes family and friends into your home like the hearty, full-bodied aroma of baking bread emanating from the kitchen. And nothing tastes as wonderful as a loaf of homemade bread fresh from the oven.

In these busy times, however, baking your own bread seems to have become a luxury, something reserved for holidays and other special occasions. No more. With Better Homes and Gardens® Bread Machine Bounty and your bread machine, it's never been easier to bake bread.

Take advantage of this cookbook's more than 100 enticing recipes–all developed specifically for bread machines–to make homemade bread for dinner tonight. Your favorites are here and can be baked with less effort than you thought possible. You'll be able to use these tempting recipes in your machine with confidence because each one was tested for quality in the Better Homes and Gardens® Test Kitchen.

Now you can enjoy a piping-hot loaf of crusty French Bread with your family, dazzle a dinner party with the unique flavor of Walnut-Anise Bulgur Bread, or share secrets with a friend over the rich taste of Pesto and Wheat Bread.

With Bread Machine Bounty, it's simple to fill your home with the tantalizing smell and warm welcome of homemade bread.

BREAD BASICS

Recipe Testing

Every recipe in this cookbook was prepared and tested by one of eight experienced home economists in the Better Homes and Gardens® Test Kitchen. The recipes were judged on ease of preparation, texture, appeal, and flavor. No recipe can receive the Test Kitchen Seal of Approval until it meets the Test Kitchen's high standards.

The recipes for this book were tested in a variety of machines including Welbilt, Zojirushi, Hitachi, Maxim, Sanyo, Panasonic/National, Regal, and Chefmate.

Tips From the Experts in Our Test Kitchen

During the testing procedure, we discovered some basic information that you should consider when using the recipes from this book.

All ingredients should be at room temperature, unless noted otherwise in the recipe. Quickly bring about 1 cup of milk to room temperature by microwaving it on 100% (high) power about 1 minute; stir to evenly distribute heat.

Ingredients should be added to your machine according to the specific directions given in the owner's manual. Since each machine is different, we chose to list liquid ingredients first, then dry ingredients. This may not be the order the manufacturer of your specific machine recommends, so it's important to follow the directions in the manual. Any ingredients listed after the yeast, such as dried fruit or nuts, should be added at the raisin bread cycle if your machine has one. If it does not, add them according to the manufacturer's directions.

You'll notice most of the recipes in this book call for 1 teaspoon of active dry yeast. This is often less yeast than is used in recipes supplied by bread machine manufacturers. Since one package of yeast (2½ teaspoons) is enough to make two loaves of bread conventionally and our recipes make one loaf in the bread machine, 1 teaspoon of yeast is sufficient for either a 1- or 1½-pound recipe. If you like, you may add an additional ¼ to ½ teaspoon yeast to our recipes to create a loaf of bread consistent with your taste preferences. Please be advised that additional yeast may produce a loaf of bread with an airy, sometimes uneven, texture, and may cause the bread dough to rise high and stick to the lid of your machine or run over the edges of the pan.

If you prefer to use powdered milk instead of fresh, use ⅓ cup nonfat dry milk powder for each 1 cup of water and add it with the flour. *Always use powdered milk when using the timer on your machine.*

If your machine works excessively hard during the mixing cycle, add 1 or 2 tablespoons extra liquid to the bread during the first 5 to 10 minutes of the cycle.

Measuring ingredients is crucial when baking bread. Follow these easy steps when measuring liquid and dry ingredients. *For liquid ingredients,* use a glass or clear plastic measuring cup. Place the cup on a level surface and bend down so your eye is level with the marking you wish to read. Fill the cup to the marking. Don't lift the cup off the counter to your eye; your hand is not as steady as a countertop. When using measuring spoons to measure a liquid, pour the liquid just to the top of the spoon without letting it spill over. Don't measure over the mixing bowl because the liquid could overflow from the spoon into the bowl. *For dry ingredients,* use a plastic measuring cup or spoon. Be sure to stir flour before measuring to lighten it. Gently spoon the dry ingredient into a cup or spoon, and level off the top with the straight edge of a knife or a metal spatula.

Make clean-up easy by spraying the kneading paddle of your machine with nonstick spray coating before adding ingredients and by soaking the paddle and pan in hot soapy water immediately after removing the baked bread.

Use the end of the handle of a wooden spoon to remove the kneading paddle from the hot loaf of bread.

When rolling out dough mixed in a machine, stop and let the bread rest about 5 minutes; then finish rolling it out. The dough is very elastic and letting it rest makes it easier to shape.

To store baked bread, cool it completely; it will take several hours. Wrap it in foil or plastic wrap, or place it in a plastic bag. Store it in a cool, dry place up to 3 days. To freeze yeast bread, place bread in a freezer bag or container, or tightly wrap it in heavy foil. Freeze it up to 3 months. Bread can be thawed in the package for 1 hour or wrapped in foil and reheated in a 300° oven about 20 minutes.

Deciphering the Recipe Method

Recipes that give ingredients for both the 1 and 1½ pound loaf sizes use brackets [ ] to indicate recipe directions that apply only to the 1½ pound recipe.

Nutrition Calculations

You can keep track of your daily nutrition needs by using the nutrition analysis provided at the end of each recipe. For this book, the calculations are for one serving of the 1 pound loaf. (Each 1 pound loaf makes 16 servings unless noted otherwise.) When a recipe gives an ingredient substitution, the first choice is used in the analysis. Optional ingredients aren't included in the calculations.

Glossary

Barley: A cereal grain with a mild, starchy flavor and a slightly chewy texture. Pearl barley, the most popular form used for cooking, has the outer hull removed and has been polished or "pearled." It is sold in regular and quick-cooking forms. Store barley in an airtight container in a cool, dry place for up to 1 year.

Bread Flour: Flour made entirely from hard wheat, which is high in protein and well-suited to making yeast breads. Store bread flour in an airtight container in a cool, dry place for up to 5 months. For longer storage, keep it in the refrigerator or freezer.

Buckwheat Flour: Flour made of ground buckwheat groats (whole, unpolished, unroasted buckwheat kernels). There are two grades of buckwheat flour. Light buckwheat flour is ground with very little hull; it has a delicate flavor and is light in color. Dark buckwheat flour is ground with the hull and has a strong flavor. Store buckwheat flour in an airtight container in a cool, dry place for up to 5 months. For longer storage, keep it in the refrigerator or freezer.

Bulgur: A parched, cracked wheat product. To make it, the whole wheat kernel is soaked, cooked, and dried. Then 5 percent of the bran is removed from the dried, hard wheat kernels, and the remaining kernel is cracked into small pieces. It has a delicate, nutty flavor. Store bulgur in an airtight container in a cool, dry place for up to 6 months or in the freezer indefinitely.

Cornmeal: Dried yellow, blue, or white corn kernels that have been finely ground. Cornmeal labeled "stone ground" is slightly coarser than other cornmeal. Store cornmeal in an airtight container in a cool, dry place for up to 6 months or in the refrigerator or freezer for up to 1 year.

Cracked Wheat: Coarsely ground, unpolished whole wheat kernels. It has a nutty flavor and crunchy texture. Store cracked wheat in an airtight container in a cool, dry place for up to 6 months or freeze for up to 1 year.

Gluten Flour: Flour made by removing most of the starch from high-protein, hard-wheat flour, leaving a product high in gluten. (Gluten is an elastic protein present in all flours.) It helps breads, especially those made with low-gluten flours, to hold together. Gluten flour also may be called gluten. It should be stored in the same manner as other flours.

Millet: A cereal grain with tiny, round, yellow kernels. It tastes slightly nutty and has a chewy texture. Store millet in an airtight container in a cool, dry place for up to 2 years.

Oats: The cereal grain produced by the cereal grass of the same name. Oats have a nutty flavor and chewy texture and must be hulled before they can be eaten. Whole oats minus the hulls are called groats. Rolled or old-fashioned oats are oat groats that have been steamed then flattened by steel rollers into flakes. Quick-cooking oats are oat groats that are cut into several pieces before rolling to shorten the cooking time. Store oats in an airtight container in a cool, dry place for up to 6 months or in the freezer for 1 year.

Wheat Berries: Whole wheat kernels with just the hulls removed. Store wheat berries in an airtight container in a cool, dry place for up to 6 months or freeze for up to 1 year.

Wheat Bran: The outer layer of the wheat kernel. It comes in plain and toasted forms and also is known as miller's bran. Store wheat bran in an airtight container in a cool, dry place for up to 1 month, refrigerate for up to 3 months, or freeze for up to 1 year.

Wheat Germ: The embryo or sprouting section of the wheat kernel. It is sold both raw and toasted. Wheat germ is extremely perishable. Keep it in the refrigerator for up to 3 months.

Whole Wheat Flour: A coarse-textured flour ground from the entire wheat kernel. It also is called graham flour. Store whole wheat flour in an airtight container in a cool, dry place for up to 5 months. For longer storage, keep it in the refrigerator or freezer.

Wild Rice: The long, dark brown or black, nutty-flavored seed of an annual marsh grass. It actually is not rice, but a cereal grain. Store uncooked wild rice indefinitely in a cool, dry place or in the refrigerator.

Yeast: A tiny, single-celled organism. Yeast feeds on the sugar in dough, producing carbon dioxide gas that makes the dough rise. Active dry yeast is simply dried granules of yeast. Store packages of dry yeast in a cool, dry place and the yeast will stay fresh until the expiration date stamped on the package. Store open jars of yeast tightly covered in the refrigerator. Use before the expiration date printed on the jar.

Mail-Order Sources:

If you're having difficulty locating specialty ingredients, try the mail-order sources listed below. Many of the companies have catalogs to help you obtain the items you need.

American Spoon Foods
1668 Clarion Avenue
P.O. Box 566
Petoskey, MI 49770-0566
(616-347-9030 or 800-222-5886)

Carries dried cherries, blueberries, and cranberries; preserves and jellies; and nuts.

Country Cherry De-Lites—Country Ovens, Ltd.
123 Main Street
P.O. Box 195
Forestville, WI 54213
(414-743-2330)

Offers dried cherries and cranberries.

Fiesta Nut Corporation
P.O. Box 366
75 Harbor Road
Port Washington, NY 11050
(516-883-1403 or 800-645-3296)

Carries nuts, sunflower seeds, pumpkin seeds, and dried fruits.

Jaffe Bros. Inc.
P.O. Box 636
Valley Center, CA 92082
(619-749-1133 or Fax 619-749-1282)

Offers a variety of organic grains and grain products including unusual, hard-to-find items. They also carry a selection of dried fruits, nuts, and seeds.

Morgan's Mills
RD 2, Box 4602
Union, ME 04862
(207-785-4900 or Fax 207-785-4907)

Carries the following flours: bread, whole wheat bread, pastry, whole wheat pastry, oat, barley, rye, corn, millet, buckwheat, and brown rice.

The Vermont Country Store
P.O. Box 3000
Manchester Center, VT 05255-3000
(802-362-2400)

Offers stone-ground flours and cereals.

War Eagle Mill
Rte. 5, Box 411
Rogers, AR 72756
(501-789-5343)

Produces stone-ground flours and meals from certified organic grains. Products include yellow and white cornmeal, cracked wheat, wheat bran, wheat germ, whole wheat flour, buckwheat flour, and rye flour.

Bread Spreads

Enhance your homemade bread's flavor with a flavored butter. These butters will keep for up to 2 weeks in the refrigerator or for 1 month in the freezer.
To make any of the following recipes, start with ½ cup softened butter or margarine.

Tomato-Pepper Butter
Stir in ¼ cup finely snipped dried tomatoes (oil-pack) and ½ teaspoon cracked black pepper.

Roasted Red Pepper Butter
With an electric mixer, beat in ¼ cup chopped, canned, roasted sweet red peppers or pimiento and 1 or 2 cloves garlic, minced. Stir again before serving.

Sesame Butter
Stir in 4 teaspoons toasted sesame seed.

Lemon Butter
Stir in ½ teaspoon finely shredded lemon peel and 2 teaspoons lemon juice.

Wine-Tarragon Butter
With an electric mixer, beat in 2 tablespoons snipped, fresh tarragon or dillweed or ½ teaspoon dried tarragon, crushed, or dried dillweed, and 2 tablespoons dry white wine or dry sherry.

Mustard-Sage Butter
Stir in 2 tablespoons snipped, fresh sage or ½ teaspoon dried sage, crushed, and 2 to 4 teaspoons Dijon-style or prepared mustard.

Parmesan Butter
Stir in 2 tablespoons grated Parmesan cheese and 1 tablespoon snipped, fresh basil or ½ teaspoon dried basil, crushed.

Citrus Butter
Stir in 1 tablespoon powdered sugar and ½ teaspoon finely shredded orange or lemon peel.

Breakfast Butter
Stir in 2 tablespoons honey or maple-flavored syrup.

Cinnamon Butter
Stir in 1 tablespoon powdered sugar and ¼ teaspoon ground cinnamon.

WHITE BREADS

White Bread 17

Potato Bread 18

Buttermilk-Oatmeal Bread 19

Jalapeño, Cheddar, and Corn Bread 20

Onion-Pepper Bread 21

Garlic and Chive Bread 22

Roasted Pepper Bread with Cilantro 23

Curried Bread 24

Anadama Bread 25

Sweet Potato and Apple Bread 26

WHITE BREAD

1 Pound	Ingredients	1½ Pound
¾ cup	**milk**	1¼ cups
1½ teaspoons	**shortening**	2 teaspoons
2 cups	**bread flour**	3 cups
2 teaspoons	**sugar**	1 tablespoon
½ teaspoon	**salt**	½ teaspoon
1 teaspoon	**active dry yeast *or* bread machine yeast**	1 teaspoon

Add ingredients to machine according to manufacturer's directions. Small loaf serves 16. One teaspoon yeast is recommended by our Test Kitchen for either loaf size (see page 6).

Nutrition information per serving: 74 calories, 3 g protein, 14 g carbohydrate, 1 g fat (0 g saturated), 1 mg cholesterol, 73 mg sodium, 39 mg potassium.

POTATO BREAD

1 Pound	Ingredients	1½ Pound
½ cup	water	¾ cup
⅓ cup	peeled, chopped potato	½ cup
	Buttermilk	
1½ teaspoons	margarine *or* butter	2 teaspoons
2¼ cups	bread flour	3⅓ cups
2 teaspoons	sugar	1 tablespoon
½ teaspoon	salt	¾ teaspoon
1 teaspoon	active dry yeast *or* bread machine yeast	1 teaspoon

In a small saucepan combine the water and potato. Bring to boiling; reduce heat. Cook, covered, about 8 minutes or till potato is very tender. *Do not drain.* Mash potato in the water. Measure the potato-water mixture. Add enough buttermilk to make ⅞ cup [1⅓ cups] total. Cool to room temperature. Add ingredients to machine according to manufacturer's directions. Small loaf serves 16.

One teaspoon yeast is recommended by our Test Kitchen for either loaf size (see page 6).

Nutrition information per serving: 79 calories, 3 g protein, 15 g carbohydrate, 1 g fat (0 g saturated), 0 mg cholesterol, 74 mg sodium, 38 mg potassium.

BUTTERMILK-OATMEAL BREAD

Setting 2
Normal
3 hours

1 Pound	Ingredients	1½ Pound
¾ cup	**buttermilk**	1¼ cups
1 tablespoon	**honey**	2 tablespoons
1½ teaspoons	**margarine *or* butter**	1 tablespoon
1¾ cups	**bread flour**	2¾ cups
⅓ cup	**toasted rolled oats***	¾ cup
½ teaspoon	**salt**	¾ teaspoon
1 teaspoon	**active dry yeast *or* bread machine yeast**	1 teaspoon

Add ingredients to machine according to manufacturer's directions. Small loaf serves 16.
One teaspoon yeast is recommended by our Test Kitchen for either loaf size (see page 6).

*Note: For toasted rolled oats, place oats in shallow baking pan. Bake in a 350° oven for 15 to 20 minutes or till oats are lightly browned. Cool.

Nutrition information per serving: 76 calories, 3 g protein, 14 g carbohydrate, 1 g fat (0 g saturated), 0 mg cholesterol, 83 mg sodium, 47 mg potassium.

JALAPEÑO, CHEDDAR, AND CORNBREAD

1 Pound	Ingredients	1½ Pound
¾ cup	**buttermilk**	1¼ cups
1½ teaspoons	**shortening**	2 teaspoons
2 cups	**bread flour**	3 cups
½ cup	**shredded cheddar cheese with jalapeño peppers**	¾ cup
	or **Monterey Jack cheese with jalapeño peppers**	
⅓ cup	**cornmeal**	½ cup
2 teaspoons	**sugar**	1 tablespoon
½ teaspoon	**salt**	¾ teaspoon
1 teaspoon	**active dry yeast *or* bread machine yeast**	1 teaspoon

Add ingredients to machine according to manufacturer's directions. Small loaf serves 16. One teaspoon yeast is recommended by our Test Kitchen for either loaf size (see page 6).

Nutrition information per serving: 97 calories, 4 g protein, 16 g carbohydrate, 2 g fat (1 g saturated), 4 mg cholesterol, 101 mg sodium, 47 mg potassium.

ONION-PEPPER BREAD

1 Pound	Ingredients	1½ Pound
1 cup	**chopped onion**	1½ cups
1 clove	**garlic, minced**	1 clove
1 tablespoon	**margarine *or* butter**	2 tablespoons
¾ cup	**milk**	1¼ cups
2 cups	**bread flour**	3 cups
2 teaspoons	**sugar**	1 tablespoon
½ teaspoon	**salt**	¾ teaspoon
¼ to ½ teaspoon	**coarsely ground pepper**	½ to ¾ teaspoon
Dash	**ground red pepper**	⅛ teaspoon
1 teaspoon	**active dry yeast *or* bread machine yeast**	1 teaspoon

In a medium skillet cook onion and garlic in hot margarine or butter till onion is tender but not brown, stirring occasionally. Cool slightly. Add ingredients to machine according to manufacturer's directions, adding the onion-margarine mixture with milk. Small loaf serves 16.

One teaspoon yeast is recommended by our Test Kitchen for either loaf size (see page 6).

Nutrition information per serving: 88 calories, 3 g protein, 15 g carbohydrate, 2 g fat (0 g saturated), 1 mg cholesterol, 90 mg sodium, 59 mg potassium.

GARLIC AND CHIVE BREAD

1 Pound	Ingredients	1½ Pound
3 cloves	garlic, minced	5 cloves
2 teaspoons	margarine *or* butter	1 tablespoon
¾ cup	milk	1¼ cups
2 cups	bread flour	3 cups
¼ cup	grated Parmesan cheese	⅓ cup
4 teaspoons	snipped fresh chives	2 tablespoons
2 teaspoons	sugar	1 tablespoon
½ teaspoon	salt	¾ teaspoon
1 teaspoon	active dry yeast *or* bread machine yeast	1 teaspoon

In a small skillet cook garlic in hot margarine or butter over medium heat for 30 seconds. Cool slightly. Add ingredients to machine according to manufacturer's directions. Small loaf serves 16.

One teaspoon yeast is recommended by our Test Kitchen for either loaf size (see page 6).

Nutrition information per serving: 82 calories, 3 g protein, 14 g carbohydrate, 1 g fat (1 g saturated), 2 mg cholesterol, 108 mg sodium, 44 mg potassium.

ROASTED PEPPER BREAD WITH CILANTRO

1 Pound	Ingredients	1½ Pound
¾ cup	milk	1¼ cups
1 small (⅓ cup)	red pepper, roasted and chopped*	1 medium (½ cup)
1½ teaspoons	shortening	2 teaspoons
2 cups	bread flour	3 cups
2 teaspoons	sugar	1 tablespoon
2 teaspoons	snipped fresh cilantro	2 teaspoons
	or ½ teaspoon dried cilantro	
½ teaspoon	garlic salt	¾ teaspoon
1 teaspoon	active dry yeast *or* bread machine yeast	1 teaspoon

Add ingredients to machine according to manufacturer's directions, adding the roasted red pepper with the milk. Small loaf serves 16.

One teaspoon yeast is recommended by our Test Kitchen for either loaf size (see page 6).

*Note: To roast red pepper, halve pepper and remove stem, seeds, and membrane. Place pepper halves, cut sides down, on a foil-lined baking sheet. Bake in a 425° oven for 20 to 25 minutes or till skin is bubbly and browned. Place pepper halves in a new brown paper bag; seal and let stand for 20 to 30 minutes or till cool enough to handle. Peel skin from pepper. Discard skin; chop pepper.

Nutrition information per serving: 75 calories, 3 g protein, 14 g carbohydrate, 1 g fat (0 g saturated), 1 mg cholesterol, 70 mg sodium, 46 mg potassium.

CURRIED BREAD

1 Pound	Ingredients	1½ Pound
⅓ cup	chopped onion	½ cup
1 teaspoon	curry powder	1½ teaspoons
1 tablespoon	margarine *or* butter	2 tablespoons
¾ cup	milk	1¼ cups
2 cups	bread flour	3 cups
2 teaspoons	sugar	1 tablespoon
½ teaspoon	salt	¾ teaspoon
1 teaspoon	active dry yeast *or* bread machine yeast	1 teaspoon
¼ cup	coconut	⅓ cup
¼ cup	chopped peanuts	⅓ cup
¼ cup	snipped raisins	⅓ cup

In a small saucepan cook onion and curry powder in hot margarine or butter till onion is tender. Cool slightly. Add ingredients to machine according to manufacturer's directions. Small loaf serves 16.

One teaspoon yeast is recommended by our Test Kitchen for either loaf size (see page 6).

Nutrition information per serving: 103 calories, 3 g protein, 17 g carbohydrate, 3 g fat (1 g saturated), 1 mg cholesterol, 82 mg sodium, 83 mg potassium.

ANADAMA BREAD

1 Pound	Ingredients	1½ Pound
¾ cup	water	1¼ cups
3 tablespoons	dark molasses	¼ cup
2 tablespoons	shortening	3 tablespoons
2 cups	bread flour	3 cups
⅓ cup	cornmeal	½ cup
½ teaspoon	salt	¾ teaspoon
¾ teaspoon	active dry yeast *or* bread machine yeast	1 teaspoon

Add ingredients to machine according to manufacturer's directions. Small loaf serves 16.
One teaspoon yeast is recommended by our Test Kitchen for either loaf size (see page 6).

Nutrition information per serving: 96 calories, 2 g protein, 17 g carbohydrate, 2 g fat (0 g saturated), 0 mg cholesterol, 68 mg sodium, 60 mg potassium.

Sweet Potato and Apple Bread

1 Pound	Ingredients	1½ Pound
½ cup	water	¾ cup
⅓ cup	peeled, chopped sweet potato	½ cup
	Milk	
¾ cup	peeled, shredded apple	1 cup
1½ teaspoons	margarine *or* butter	2 teaspoons
2⅓ cups	bread flour	3½ cups
2 teaspoons	brown sugar	1 tablespoon
½ teaspoon	salt	¾ teaspoon
¾ teaspoon	active dry yeast *or* bread machine yeast	1 teaspoon

In a small saucepan combine the water and potato. Bring to boiling; reduce heat. Cook, covered, about 8 minutes or till very tender. *Do not drain.* Mash potato in the water. Measure the potato-water mixture. Add enough milk to make ⅔ cup [1 cup] total. Cool to room temperature. Add ingredients to machine according to manufacturer's directions. Small loaf serves 16.

One teaspoon yeast is recommended by our Test Kitchen for either loaf size (see page 6).

Nutrition information per serving: 84 calories, 3 g protein, 17 g carbohydrate, 1 g fat (0 g saturated), 0 mg cholesterol, 73 mg sodium, 46 mg potassium.

WHEAT BREADS

Whole Wheat Bread 28
Millet and Wheat Bread...................29
Wheat 'n' Seed Bread 30
Pepper and Fennel Loaf.................. 31
Granary Bread 32
Buckwheat Bread 33
Sprouted Wheat Loaf...................... 34
Spiced Wheat and Honey Loaf........ 35
Walnut-Anise Bulgur Bread 36
Maple and Wheat Nut Bread 37
Three-Grain Bread 38
Sage Wheat Bread 39
Pesto and Wheat Bread 40
Chili Bread 41
Italian Cheese Bread....................... 42
Bacon-Chive Bread 43
Wild Rice and Oat Bread 44
Cracked Wheat and Basil Bread 45
Olive Loaf 46

Barley and Corn Bread 47
Dried Tomato and Pine Nut Bread ...48
Eggplant Bread 49
Carrot-Ginger Wheat Bread 50
Mushroom-Leek Bread 51
Wheat 'n' Zucchini Bread 52
Lemon-Cheese Wheat Bread 53
Apricot-Sesame Wheat Bread 54
Blueberry-Granola Wheat Bread 55
Orange and Fennel Wheat Bread 56
Pineapple-Carrot Bread 57
Spiced Maple and Cranberry Bread ..58
Herb-Currant Bread 59
Apple-Wheat Bread 60
Rhubarb Bread 61
Pear and Blue Cheese Bread 62
Peaches and Cream Pistachio
    Bread 63

WHOLE WHEAT BREAD

1 Pound	Ingredients	1½ Pound
¾ cup plus 2 tablespoons	milk	1¼ cups
1½ teaspoons	shortening	2 teaspoons
1⅓ cups	whole wheat flour	2 cups
⅔ cup	bread flour	1 cup
2 teaspoons	brown sugar	1 tablespoon
½ teaspoon	salt	¾ teaspoon
1 teaspoon	active dry yeast *or* bread machine yeast	1 teaspoon

Add ingredients to machine according to manufacturer's directions. Small loaf serves 16. One teaspoon yeast is recommended by our Test Kitchen for either loaf size (see page 6).

Nutrition information per serving: 67 calories, 3 g protein, 13 g carbohydrate, 1 g fat (0 g saturated), 1 mg cholesterol, 74 mg sodium, 73 mg potassium.

MILLET AND WHEAT BREAD

1 Pound	Ingredients	1½ Pound
3 tablespoons	millet	¼ cup
¾ cup plus 2 tablespoons	milk	1¼ cups
1½ teaspoons	shortening	2 teaspoons
1¼ cups	whole wheat flour	1¾ cups
⅔ cup	bread flour	1 cup
2 teaspoons	brown sugar	1 tablespoon
½ teaspoon	salt	¾ teaspoon
1 teaspoon	active dry yeast *or* bread machine yeast	1 teaspoon

Place millet in a small mixing bowl. Pour enough boiling water over millet to cover it. Let it soak 5 minutes. Drain well. Add ingredients to machine according to manufacturer's directions. Small loaf serves 16.

One teaspoon yeast is recommended by our Test Kitchen for either loaf size (see page 6).

Nutrition information per serving: 74 calories, 3 g protein, 14 g carbohydrate, 1 g fat (0 g saturated), 1 mg cholesterol, 74 mg sodium, 75 mg potassium.

WHEAT 'N' SEED BREAD

1 Pound	Ingredients	1½ Pound
¾ cup plus 2 tablespoons	milk	1¼ cup
1 tablespoon	honey	2 tablespoons
1½ teaspoons	shortening	2 teaspoons
1⅓ cups	whole wheat flour	2 cups
⅔ cup	bread flour	1 cup
¼ cup	sunflower seeds	⅓ cup
4 teaspoons	sesame seed	2 tablespoons
1 teaspoon	poppy seed	2 teaspoons
½ teaspoon	salt	¾ teaspoon
1 teaspoon	active dry yeast *or* bread machine yeast	1 teaspoon

Add ingredients to machine according to manufacturer's directions, adding the sunflower seeds, sesame seed, and poppy seed with the flour. Small loaf serves 16.

One teaspoon yeast is recommended by our Test Kitchen for either loaf size (see page 6).

Nutrition information per serving: 81 calories, 3 g protein, 14 g carbohydrate, 3 g fat (0 g saturated), 1 mg cholesterol, 74 mg sodium, 92 mg potassium.

PEPPER AND FENNEL LOAF

1 Pound	Ingredients	1½ Pound
¾ cup plus 2 tablespoons	milk	1¼ cups
1½ teaspoons	shortening	2 teaspoons
1⅓ cups	whole wheat flour	2 cups
⅔ cup	bread flour	1 cup
2 teaspoons	brown sugar	1 tablespoon
½ teaspoon	salt	¾ teaspoon
½ teaspoon	fennel seed	1 teaspoon
¼ to ½ teaspoon	coarsely ground black pepper	½ to 1 teaspoon
1 teaspoon	active dry yeast *or* bread machine yeast	1 teaspoon

Add ingredients to machine according to manufacturer's directions. Small loaf serves 16. One teaspoon yeast is recommended by our Test Kitchen for either loaf size (see page 6).

Nutrition information per serving: 48 calories, 2 g protein, 9 g carbohydrate, 1 g fat (0 g saturated), 1 mg cholesterol, 74 mg sodium, 39 mg potassium.

GRANARY BREAD

1 Pound	Ingredients	1½ Pound
3 tablespoons	cracked wheat	¼ cup
3 tablespoons	millet	¼ cup
1 cup	boiling water	1 cup
¾ cup plus 2 tablespoons	water	1¼ cups
1 tablespoon	molasses *or* honey	2 tablespoons
1½ teaspoons	shortening	2 teaspoons
1⅓ cups	whole wheat flour	2 cups
⅔ cup	bread flour	1 cup
3 tablespoons	rolled oats	¼ cup
2 tablespoons	cornmeal	3 tablespoons
1 tablespoon	toasted wheat germ *or* unprocessed wheat bran	2 tablespoons
2 teaspoons	gluten flour	1 tablespoon
½ teaspoon	salt	¾ teaspoon
1 teaspoon	active dry yeast *or* bread machine yeast	1 teaspoon

Place cracked wheat and millet in a small mixing bowl. Add the 1 cup boiling water. Let it soak 5 minutes. Drain well. Add ingredients to machine according to manufacturer's directions. Small loaf serves 16.

One teaspoon yeast is recommended by our Test Kitchen for either loaf size (see page 6).

Nutrition information per serving: 83 calories, 3 g protein, 16 g carbohydrate, 1 g fat (0 g saturated), 0 mg cholesterol, 69 mg sodium, 81 mg potassium.

BUCKWHEAT BREAD

1 Pound	Ingredients	1½ Pound
¾ cup	water	1¼ cups
1 tablespoon	shortening	1 tablespoon
1⅓ cups	bread flour	2 cups
1 cup	buckwheat flour	1½ cups
1 tablespoon	gluten flour (optional)	2 tablespoons
1 tablespoon	brown sugar	2 tablespoons
½ teaspoon	salt	¾ teaspoon
1 teaspoon	active dry yeast *or* bread machine yeast	1 teaspoon

Add ingredients to machine according to manufacturer's directions. Small loaf serves 16. One teaspoon yeast is recommended by our Test Kitchen for either loaf size (see page 6).

Nutrition information per serving: 77 calories, 2 g protein, 14 g carbohydrate, 1 g fat (0 g saturated), 0 mg cholesterol, 68 mg sodium, 62 mg potassium.

SPROUTED WHEAT LOAF

1 Pound	Ingredients	1½ Pound
1 cup	water	1¼ cups
1½ teaspoons	shortening	2 teaspoons
1⅓ cups	whole wheat flour	2 cups
⅔ cup	bread flour	1 cup
⅔ cup	chopped sprouts*	1 cup
4 teaspoons	toasted wheat germ	2 tablespoons
1 tablespoon	brown sugar	2 tablespoons
½ teaspoon	salt	¾ teaspoon
1 teaspoon	active dry yeast *or* bread machine yeast	1 teaspoon

Add ingredients to machine according to manufacturer's directions. Small loaf serves 16. One teaspoon yeast is recommended by our Test Kitchen for either loaf size (see page 6).

Sprouts: Thoroughly wash ⅓ cup wheat berries, rye berries, or brown rice. Place the grain in a bowl and cover it with enough water (about 1 inch) for the grain to swell; cover. Let stand overnight in a cool place. Drain and rinse grain.

Wash three 1-quart jars; place about ¼ cup of the soaked grain in each jar. Cover tops of jars with two layers of cheesecloth or nylon netting. Fasten the cheesecloth on each jar with two rubber bands or a screw-top canning-jar lid band.

Place the jars on their sides in a warm, dark place (68° to 75° F). Once a day, rinse the grain by pouring lukewarm water into the jars. Swirl to moisten all the grain, then pour off the water to drain well. In 3 or 4 days, the grain should sprout. (Brown rice may take 5 to 6 days to sprout.) Once the grain has sprouted, keep it refrigerated till you need it.

Nutrition information per serving: 51 calories, 2 g protein, 10 g carbohydrate, 1 g fat (0 g saturated), 0 mg cholesterol, 69 mg sodium, 60 mg potassium.

SPICED WHEAT AND HONEY LOAF

1 Pound	Ingredients	1½ Pound
¾ cup	milk	1 cup
2 tablespoons	honey	3 tablespoons
1½ teaspoons	shortening	2 teaspoons
1⅓ cups	whole wheat flour	2 cups
⅔ cup	bread flour	1 cup
½ teaspoon	salt	¾ teaspoon
¼ teaspoon	ground cinnamon	½ teaspoon
¼ teaspoon	ground cardamom	½ teaspoon
	Dash ground cloves	
1 teaspoon	active dry yeast *or* bread machine yeast	1 teaspoon
⅓ cup	dried currants *or* raisins	½ cup

Add ingredients to machine according to manufacturer's directions. Small loaf serves 16.
One teaspoon yeast is recommended by our Test Kitchen for either loaf size (see page 6).

Nutrition information per serving: 81 calories, 3 g protein, 16 g carbohydrate, 1 g fat (0 g saturated), 1 mg cholesterol, 73 mg sodium, 97 mg potassium.

WALNUT-ANISE BULGUR BREAD

1 Pound	Ingredients	1½ Pound
¼ cup	**bulgur wheat**	⅓ cup
½ cup	**boiling water**	¾ cup
¾ cup	**milk**	1 cup plus 1 tablespoon
1½ teaspoons	**shortening**	2 teaspoons
1⅓ cups	**whole wheat flour**	2 cups
⅔ cup	**bread flour**	1 cup
¼ cup	**toasted chopped walnuts**	⅓ cup
2 teaspoons	**brown sugar**	1 tablespoon
¾ teaspoon	**aniseed, crushed**	¾ teaspoon
½ teaspoon	**salt**	¾ teaspoon
1 teaspoon	**active dry yeast *or* bread machine yeast**	1 teaspoon

Place bulgur wheat in a small mixing bowl. Add ½ cup (¾ cup) boiling water. Let it soak 5 minutes. Drain well; cool slightly. Add ingredients to machine according to manufacturer's directions, adding the bulgur wheat with the milk. Small loaf serves 16.

One teaspoon yeast is recommended by our Test Kitchen for either loaf size (see page 6).

Nutrition information per serving: 86 calories, 3 g protein, 15 g carbohydrate, 2 g fat (0 g saturated), 1 mg cholesterol, 74 mg sodium, 90 mg potassium.

MAPLE AND WHEAT NUT BREAD

1 Pound	Ingredients	1½ Pound
¾ cup	milk	1 cup
2 tablespoons	maple-flavored syrup	3 tablespoons
1½ teaspoons	shortening	2 teaspoons
1⅓ cups	whole wheat flour	2 cups
⅔ cup	bread flour	1 cup
⅓ cup	toasted chopped pecans *or* walnuts	½ cup
½ teaspoon	salt	¾ teaspoon
1 teaspoon	active dry yeast *or* bread machine yeast	1 teaspoon

Add ingredients to machine according to manufacturer's directions, adding the nuts with the flour. Small loaf serves 16.

One teaspoon yeast is recommended by our Test Kitchen for either loaf size (see page 6).

Nutrition information per serving: 88 calories, 3 g protein, 14 g carbohydrate, 2 g fat (0 g saturated), 1 mg cholesterol, 77 mg sodium, 77 mg potassium.

THREE-GRAIN BREAD

1 Pound	Ingredients	1½ Pound
2 tablespoons	barley (regular, not quick-cooking barley)	3 tablespoons
½ cup	regular rolled oats	¾ cup
¾ cup plus 2 tablespoons	milk	1¼ cups
1½ teaspoons	shortening	2 teaspoons
1 cup	bread flour	1½ cups
⅔ cup	whole wheat flour	1 cup
2 teaspoons	brown sugar	1 tablespoon
½ teaspoon	salt	¾ teaspoon
1 teaspoon	active dry yeast *or* bread machine yeast	1 teaspoon

Spread barley in a shallow baking pan. Bake in a 350° oven for 15 minutes, stirring once or twice. Let barley cool. Place the barley and rolled oats in a blender container. Cover and blend till mixture is the consistency of flour. Add ingredients to machine according to manufacturer's directions. Small loaf serves 16.

One teaspoon yeast is recommended by our Test Kitchen for either loaf size (see page 6).

Nutrition information per serving: 76 calories, 3 g protein, 14 g carbohydrate, 1 g fat (0 g saturated), 1 mg cholesterol, 74 mg sodium, 69 mg potassium.

SAGE WHEAT BREAD

1 Pound	Ingredients	1½ Pound
1 cup	milk	1⅓ cups
1½ teaspoons	shortening	1 tablespoon
1⅓ cups	whole wheat flour	2 cups
⅔ cup	bread flour	1 cup
¼ cup	cornmeal	⅓ cup
2 teaspoons	brown sugar	1 tablespoon
1½ teaspoons	snipped fresh sage *or*	2 teaspoons
	¼ teaspoon dried sage, crushed	
½ teaspoon	salt	¾ teaspoon
1 teaspoon	active dry yeast *or* bread machine yeast	1 teaspoon

Add ingredients to machine according to manufacturer's directions. Small loaf serves 16. One teaspoon yeast is recommended by our Test Kitchen for either loaf size (see page 6).

Nutrition information per serving: 76 calories, 3 g protein, 14 g carbohydrate, 1 g fat (0 g saturated), 1 mg cholesterol, 75 mg sodium, 80 mg potassium.

PESTO AND WHEAT BREAD

1 Pound	Ingredients	1½ Pound
¾ cup plus 2 tablespoons	water	1¼ cups
1 tablespoon	cooking oil	2 tablespoons
1⅓ cups	whole wheat flour	2 cups
⅔ cup	bread flour	1 cup
⅓ cup	snipped fresh basil	½ cup
¼ cup	grated Parmesan cheese	⅓ cup
3 tablespoons	oat bran	¼ cup
2 teaspoons	brown sugar	1 tablespoon
½ teaspoon	salt	¾ teaspoon
1 teaspoon	active dry yeast *or* bread machine yeast	1 teaspoon
⅓ cup	toasted pine nuts *or* slivered almonds	½ cup

Add ingredients to machine according to manufacturer's directions. Small loaf serves 16. One teaspoon yeast is recommended by our Test Kitchen for either loaf size (see page 6).

Nutrition information per serving: 92 calories, 4 g protein, 13 g carbohydrate, 3 g fat (1 g saturated), 1 mg cholesterol, 97 mg sodium, 84 mg potassium.

CHILI BREAD

1 Pound	Ingredients	1½ Pound
¼ cup	chopped onion	⅓ cup
¼ cup	chopped green pepper	⅓ cup
1 tablespoon	cooking oil	4 teaspoons
1 teaspoon	chili powder	1¼ teaspoons
¼ teaspoon	ground cumin	½ teaspoon
⅔ cup	milk	1 cup
⅓ cup	canned red kidney beans, drained	½ cup
1⅓ cups	whole wheat flour	2 cups
⅔ cup	bread flour	1 cup
2 teaspoons	brown sugar	1 tablespoon
½ teaspoon	salt	¾ teaspoon
1 teaspoon	active dry yeast *or* bread machine yeast	1 teaspoon

In a medium skillet cook onion and green pepper in hot oil till onion is tender. Add chili powder and cumin; cook 1 minute more. Cool slightly. Add ingredients to machine according to manufacturer's directions, adding the onion mixture and beans with milk. Small loaf serves 16.

One teaspoon yeast is recommended by our Test Kitchen for either loaf size (see page 6).

Nutrition information per serving: 76 calories, 3 g protein, 14 g carbohydrate, 1 g fat (0 g saturated), 1 mg cholesterol, 83 mg sodium, 87 mg potassium.

ITALIAN CHEESE BREAD

1 Pound	Ingredients	1½ Pound
¾ cup	milk	1¼ cups
⅓ cup	ricotta cheese	½ cup
1⅓ cups	whole wheat flour	2 cups
⅔ cup	bread flour	1 cup
3 tablespoons	grated Parmesan cheese	¼ cup
2 teaspoons	brown sugar	1 tablespoon
½ teaspoon	salt	¾ teaspoon
½ teaspoon	dried Italian seasoning, crushed	¾ teaspoon
1 teaspoon	active dry yeast *or* bread machine yeast	1 teaspoon

Add ingredients to machine according to manufacturer's directions. Small loaf serves 16. One teaspoon yeast is recommended by our Test Kitchen for either loaf size (see page 6).

Nutrition information per serving: 75 calories, 4 g protein, 13 g carbohydrate, 1 g fat (1 g saturated), 3 mg cholesterol, 101 mg sodium, 78 mg potassium.

Bacon-chive Bread

1 Pound	Ingredients	1½ Pound
¾ cup plus 2 tablespoons	milk	1¼ cups
4 teaspoons	prepared mustard	2 tablespoons
1½ teaspoons	shortening	1 tablespoon
1⅓ cups	whole wheat flour	2 cups
⅔ cup	bread flour	1 cup
2 teaspoons	brown sugar	1 tablespoon
½ teaspoon	salt	¾ teaspoon
1 teaspoon	active dry yeast *or* bread machine yeast	1 teaspoon
¼ cup	cooked bacon pieces	⅓ cup
2 tablespoons	snipped fresh chives	3 tablespoons

Add ingredients to machine according to manufacturer's directions. Store cooled bread in the refrigerator. Small loaf serves 16.

One teaspoon yeast is recommended by our Test Kitchen for either loaf size (see page 6).

Nutrition information per serving: 76 calories, 3 g protein, 13 g carbohydrate, 1 g fat (0 g saturated), 1 mg cholesterol, 132 mg sodium, 76 mg potassium.

WILD RICE AND OAT BRAN BREAD

1 Pound	Ingredients	1½ Pound
¾ cup	milk	1 cup
½ cup	cooked wild rice	¾ cup
1 tablespoon	shortening	2 tablespoons
1 tablespoon	honey	2 tablespoons
1⅓ cups	whole wheat flour	2 cups
⅔ cup	bread flour	1 cup
¼ cup	oat bran	⅓ cup
½ teaspoon	salt	¾ teaspoon
1 teaspoon	active dry yeast *or* bread machine yeast	1 teaspoon

Add ingredients to machine according to manufacturer's directions, adding the rice with the milk. Small loaf serves 16.

One teaspoon yeast is recommended by our Test Kitchen for either loaf size (see page 6).

Nutrition information per serving: 84 calories, 3 g protein, 15 g carbohydrate, 1 g fat (0 g saturated), 1 mg cholesterol, 75 mg sodium, 88 mg potassium.

CRACKED WHEAT AND BASIL BREAD

1 Pound	Ingredients	1½ Pound
1 cup	buttermilk	1½ cups
1 tablespoon	shortening	2 tablespoons
1⅓ cups	whole wheat flour	2 cups
⅔ cup	bread flour	1 cup
¼ cup	cracked wheat	⅓ cup
3 tablespoons	snipped fresh basil *or*	¼ cup
	½ teaspoon dried basil, crushed	
2 teaspoons	brown sugar	1 tablespoon
½ teaspoon	salt	¾ teaspoon
1 teaspoon	active dry yeast *or* bread machine yeast	1 teaspoon

Add ingredients to machine according to manufacturer's directions. Small loaf serves 16.

One teaspoon yeast is recommended by our Test Kitchen for either loaf size (see page 6).

Nutrition information per serving: 81 calories, 3 g protein, 15 g carbohydrate, 1 g fat (0 g saturated), 1 mg cholesterol, 84 mg sodium, 89 mg potassium.

OLIVE LOAF

1 Pound	Ingredients	1½ Pound
¾ cup	milk	1 cup plus 2 tablespoons
⅓ cup	chopped pimiento-stuffed green olives	½ cup
1½ teaspoons	olive oil	2 teaspoons
1⅓ cups	whole wheat flour	2 cups
⅔ cup	bread flour	1 cup
2 teaspoons	brown sugar	1 tablespoon
½ teaspoon	salt	¾ teaspon
1 teaspoon	active dry yeast *or* bread machine yeast	1 teaspoon
⅓ cup	toasted chopped almonds	½ cup

Add ingredients to machine according to manufacturer's directions, adding the olives with the milk. Small loaf serves 16.

One teaspoon yeast is recommended by our Test Kitchen for either loaf size (see page 6).

Nutrition information per serving: 86 calories, 3 g protein, 13 g carbohydrate, 3 g fat (0 g saturated), 1 mg cholesterol, 154 mg sodium, 92 mg potassium.

BARLEY AND CORN BREAD

1 Pound	Ingredients	1½ Pound
¼ cup	quick-cooking pearl barley	⅓ cup
¾ cup	water	1 cup
1 tablespoon	honey	2 tablespoons
1 tablespoon	cooking oil	2 tablespoons
1⅓ cups	whole wheat flour	2 cups
⅔ cup	bread flour	1 cup
¼ cup	cornmeal	⅓ cup
½ teaspoon	salt	¾ teaspoon
1 teaspoon	active dry yeast *or* bread machine yeast	1 teaspoon

Cook barley according to the package directions *just till tender.* If necessary, drain well. Cool slightly. Add ingredients to machine according to manufacturer's directions, adding the barley with the water. Small loaf serves 16.

One teaspoon yeast is recommended by our Test Kitchen for either loaf size (see page 6).

Nutrition information per serving: 86 calories, 3 g protein, 17 g carbohydrate, 1 g fat (0 g saturated), 0 mg cholesterol, 68 mg sodium, 63 mg potassium.

DRIED TOMATO AND PINE NUT BREAD

1 Pound	Ingredients	1½ Pound
¾ cup plus 2 tablespoons	milk	1¼ cups
1½ teaspoons	shortening	2 teaspoons
1⅓ cups	whole wheat flour	2 cups
⅔ cup	bread flour	1 cup
⅓ cup	toasted pine nuts	½ cup
¼ cup	drained and snipped dried tomatoes packed in oil	⅓ cup
2 teaspoons	brown sugar	1 tablespoon
½ teaspoon	salt	¾ teaspoon
1 teaspoon	active dry yeast *or* bread machine yeast	1 teaspoon

Add ingredients to machine according to manufacturer's directions. Small loaf serves 16. One teaspoon yeast is recommended by our Test Kitchen for either loaf size (see page 6).

Nutrition information per serving: 88 calories, 3 g protein, 14 g carbohydrate, 3 g fat (1 g saturated), 1 mg cholesterol, 79 mg sodium, 120 mg potassium.

EGGPLANT BREAD

Wheat Breads

1 Pound	Ingredients	1½ Pound
¾ cup	peeled and chopped eggplant	1 cup
¾ cup plus 2 tablespoons	milk	1¼ cups
1½ teaspoons	shortening	2 teaspoons
1⅓ cups	whole wheat flour	2 cups
⅔ cup	bread flour	1 cup
2 teaspoons	brown sugar	1 tablespoon
½ teaspoon	salt	¾ teaspoon
¼ teaspoon	dried oregano, crushed	½ teaspoon
⅛ teaspoon	ground cinnamon	¼ teaspoon
1 teaspoon	active dry yeast *or* bread machine yeast	1 teaspoon

In a medium saucepan cook eggplant, covered, in a small amount of boiling salted water for 5 minutes or till tender. Drain well; cool slightly. Add ingredients to machine according to manufacturer's directions. Small loaf serves 16.

One teaspoon yeast is recommended by our Test Kitchen for either loaf size (see page 6).

Nutrition information per serving: 68 calories, 3 g protein, 13 g carbohydrate, 1 g fat (0 g saturated), 1 mg cholesterol, 74 mg sodium, 81 mg potassium.

49

CARROT-GINGER WHEAT BREAD

1 Pound	Ingredients	1½ Pound
¾ cup	finely shredded carrot	1 cup
⅔ cup	milk	1 cup
1 tablespoon	shortening	2 tablespoons
1⅓ cups	whole wheat flour	2 cups
⅔ cup	bread flour	1 cup
2 tablespoons	toasted sesame seed	3 tablespoons
2 teaspoons	brown sugar	1 tablespoon
½ teaspoon	grated gingerroot *or*	¾ teaspoon
	¼ teaspoon ground ginger	
½ teaspoon	salt	¾ teaspoon
1 teaspoon	active dry yeast *or* bread machine yeast	1 teaspoon

Add ingredients to machine according to manufacturer's directions, adding the carrot with the milk. Small loaf serves 16.

One teaspoon yeast is recommended by our Test Kitchen for either loaf size (see page 6).

Nutrition information per serving: 78 calories, 3 g protein, 13 g carbohydrate, 2 g fat (0 g saturated), 1 mg cholesterol, 75 mg sodium, 89 mg potassium.

MUSHROOM-LEEK BREAD

Wheat Breads

1 Pound	Ingredients	1½ Pound
1 cup	chopped mushrooms	1½ cups
⅓ cup	thinly sliced leek	½ cup
½ teaspoon	dried rosemary, crushed	¾ teaspoon
2 tablespoons	margarine *or* butter	3 tablespoons
¾ cup	milk	1 cup plus 2 tablespoons
1⅓ cups	whole wheat flour	2 cups
⅔ cup	bread flour	1 cup
1 tablespoon	gluten flour	2 tablespoons
2 teaspoons	brown sugar	1 tablespoon
½ teaspoon	salt	¾ teaspoon
1 teaspoon	active dry yeast *or* bread machine yeast	1 teaspoon

In a large skillet cook mushrooms, leek, and rosemary in hot margarine or butter on medium-high heat for 4 to 5 minutes or till tender and most of the liquid has evaporated. Cool slightly. Add ingredients to machine according to manufacturer's directions, adding the mushroom mixture with the milk. Small loaf serves 16.

One teaspoon yeast is recommended by our Test Kitchen for either loaf size (see page 6).

Nutrition information per serving: 78 calories, 3 g protein, 13 g carbohydrate, 2 g fat (0 g saturated), 1 mg cholesterol, 91 mg sodium, 91 mg potassium.

51

WHEAT 'N' ZUCCHINI BREAD

1 Pound	Ingredients	1½ Pound
½ cup	milk	1 cup
¾ cup	coarsely shredded zucchini	1 cup
1 tablespoon	shortening	2 tablespoons
1⅓ cups	whole wheat flour	2 cups
⅔ cup	bread flour	1 cup
1 tablespoon	gluten flour	2 tablespoons
2 teaspoons	brown sugar	1 tablespoon
1 teaspoon	finely shredded lemon peel	1½ teaspoons
½ teaspoon	salt	¾ teaspoon
1 teaspoon	active dry yeast *or* bread machine yeast	1 teaspoon

Add ingredients to machine according to manufacturer's directions, adding the zucchini with the milk. Small loaf serves 16.

One teaspoon yeast is recommended by our Test Kitchen for either loaf size (see page 6).

Nutrition information per serving: 69 calories, 3 g protein, 13 g carbohydrate, 1 g fat (0 g saturated), 1 mg cholesterol, 72 mg sodium, 85 mg potassium.

LEMON-CHEESE WHEAT BREAD

Wheat Breads

1 Pound	Ingredients	1½ Pound
½ cup	milk	¾ cup
½ cup	cream-style cottage cheese	¾ cup
1½ teaspoons	shortening	2 teaspoons
1⅓ cups	whole wheat flour	2 cups
⅔ cup	bread flour	1 cup
2 teaspoons	brown sugar	1 tablespoon
2 teaspoons	finely shredded lemon peel	1 tablespoon
½ teaspoon	salt	¾ teaspoon
¼ teaspoon	dried thyme, crushed	½ teaspoon
1 teaspoon	active dry yeast *or* bread machine yeast	1 teaspoon

Add ingredients to machine according to manufacturer's directions. (Use light setting, if available.) Small loaf serves 16.

One teaspoon yeast is recommended by our Test Kitchen for either loaf size (see page 6).

Nutrition information per serving: 72 calories, 3 g protein, 13 g carbohydrate, 1 g fat (0 g saturated), 2 mg cholesterol, 98 mg sodium, 70 mg potassium.

53

APRICOT-SESAME WHEAT BREAD

1 Pound	Ingredients	1½ Pound
⅓ cup	**snipped dried apricots**	½ cup
	Boiling water	
¾ cup plus 2 tablespoons	**milk**	1¼ cups
1½ teaspoons	**shortening**	2 teaspoons
1⅛ cups	**whole wheat flour**	2 cups
⅔ cup	**bread flour**	1 cup
3 tablespoons	**toasted sesame seed**	¼ cup
2 teaspoons	**brown sugar**	1 tablespoon
½ teaspoon	**salt**	¾ teaspoon
1 teaspoon	**active dry yeast *or* bread machine yeast**	1 teaspoon

Place apricots in a small mixing bowl. Add enough boiling water to cover the apricots. Let them soak for 5 minutes. Drain well. Add ingredients to machine according to manufacturer's directions. Small loaf serves 16.

One teaspoon yeast is recommended by our Test Kitchen for either loaf size (see page 6).

Nutrition information per serving: 81 calories, 3 g protein, 14 g carbohydrate, 2 g fat (0 g saturated), 1 mg cholesterol, 75 mg sodium, 104 mg potassium.

BLUEBERRY-GRANOLA WHEAT BREAD

Wheat Breads

1 Pound	Ingredients	1½ Pound
1 cup	milk	1½ cups
1½ teaspoons	shortening	2 teaspoons
1⅓ cups	whole wheat flour	2 cups
⅔ cup	bread flour	1 cup
⅓ cup	granola	½ cup
2 teaspoons	brown sugar	1 tablespoon
½ teaspoon	salt	¾ teaspoon
1 teaspoon	active dry yeast *or* bread machine yeast	1 teaspoon
¼ cup	dried blueberries	⅓ cup

Add ingredients to machine according to manufacturer's directions. Small loaf serves 16. One teaspoon yeast is recommended by our Test Kitchen for either loaf size (see page 6).

Nutrition information per serving: 89 calories, 3 g protein, 17 g carbohydrate, 1 g fat (1 g saturated), 1 mg cholesterol, 80 mg sodium, 84 mg potassium.

ORANGE AND FENNEL WHEAT BREAD

1 Pound	Ingredients	1½ Pound
¾ cup plus 2 tablespoons	milk	1¼ cups
1½ teaspoons	shortening	2 teaspoons
1⅓ cups	whole wheat flour	2 cups
⅔ cup	bread flour	1 cup
2 teaspoons	brown sugar	1 tablespoon
2 teaspoons	finely shredded orange *or* lemon peel	1 tablespoon
¾ teaspoon	fennel seed	1 teaspoon
½ teaspoon	salt	¾ teaspoon
1 teaspoon	active dry yeast *or* bread machine yeast	1 teaspoon

Add ingredients to machine according to manufacturer's directions. Small loaf serves 16. One teaspoon yeast is recommended by our Test Kitchen for either loaf size (see page 6).

Nutrition information per serving: 68 calories, 3 g protein, 13 g carbohydrate, 1 g fat (0 g saturated), 1 mg cholesterol, 74 mg sodium, 75 mg potassium.

PINEAPPLE-CARROT BREAD

1 Pound	Ingredients	1½ Pound
⅔ cup	buttermilk	¾ cup
½ cup canned	crushed pineapple (juice pack), drained	1 8-ounce can
⅓ cup	shredded carrot	½ cup
1½ teaspoons	shortening	1 tablespoon
1⅓ cups	whole wheat flour	2 cups
⅔ cup	bread flour	1 cup
2 teaspoons	brown sugar	1 tablespoon
½ teaspoon	salt	¾ teaspoon
1 teaspoon	active dry yeast *or* bread machine yeast	1 teaspoon

Add ingredients to machine according to manufacturer's directions, adding the pineapple and carrot with buttermilk. Small loaf serves 16.

One teaspoon yeast is recommended by our Test Kitchen for either loaf size (see page 6).

Nutrition information per serving: 71 calories, 3 g protein, 14 g carbohydrate, 1 g fat (0 g saturated), 0 mg cholesterol, 79 mg sodium, 85 mg potassium.

SPICED MAPLE AND CRANBERRY BREAD

1 Pound	Ingredients	1½ Pound
¾ cup	milk	1 cup
3 tablespoons	maple-flavored syrup	¼ cup
1 tablespoon	margarine *or* butter	2 tablespoons
1⅓ cups	whole wheat flour	2 cups
⅔ cup	bread flour	1 cup
½ teaspoon	salt	¾ teaspoon
¼ teaspoon	apple pie spice	½ teaspoon
1 teaspoon	active dry yeast *or* bread machine yeast	1 teaspoon
½ cup	snipped dried cranberries	⅔ cup

Add ingredients to machine according to manufacturer's directions. (Use light setting, if available.) Small loaf serves 16.

One teaspoon yeast is recommended by our Test Kitchen for either loaf size (see page 6).

Nutrition information per serving: 90 calories, 3 g protein, 18 g carbohydrate, 1 g fat (0 g saturated), 1 mg cholesterol, 88 mg sodium, 71 mg potassium.

HERB-CURRANT BREAD

1 Pound	Ingredients	1½ Pound
1 cup	milk	1¼ cups
1 tablespoon	shortening	2 tablespoons
1⅓ cups	whole wheat flour	2 cups
⅔ cup	bread flour	1 cup
2 teaspoons	brown sugar	1 tablespoon
½ teaspoon	salt	¾ teaspoon
½ teaspoon	dried basil, crushed	¾ teaspoon
¼ teaspoon	dried thyme, crushed	½ teaspoon
¼ teaspoon	dried marjoram, crushed	¼ teaspoon
1 teaspoon	active dry yeast *or* bread machine yeast	1 teaspoon
⅓ cup	dried currants	½ cup

Add ingredients to machine according to manufacturer's directions. Small loaf serves 16. One teaspoon yeast is recommended by our Test Kitchen for either loaf size (see page 6).

Nutrition information per serving: 72 calories, 2 g protein, 13 g carbohydrate, 1 g fat (0 g saturated), 1 mg cholesterol, 75 mg sodium, 94 mg potassium.

Apple Wheat Bread

1 Pound	Ingredients	1½ Pound
⅔ cup	apple cider *or* apple juice	1 cup
1½ teaspoons	shortening	1 tablespoon
1⅓ cups	whole wheat flour	2 cups
⅔ cup	bread flour	1 cup
2 teaspoons	brown sugar	1 tablespoon
½ teaspoon	salt	¾ teaspoon
1 teaspoon	active dry yeast *or* bread machine yeast	1 teaspoon
½ cup	shredded peeled apple	¾ cup
⅓ cup	chopped cashews, peanuts, *or* walnuts	½ cup

Add ingredients to machine according to manufacturer's directions. Small loaf serves 16. One teaspoon yeast is recommended by our Test Kitchen for either loaf size (see page 6).

Nutrition information per serving: 85 calories, 3 g protein, 14 g carbohydrate, 2 g fat (0 g saturated), 0 mg cholesterol, 68 mg sodium, 89 mg potassium.

RHUBARB BREAD

1 Pound	Ingredients	1½ Pound
¾ cup	chopped rhubarb	1 cup
¾ cup	water	1 cup
¼ teaspoon	finely shredded orange peel	½ teaspoon
1 tablespoon	margarine *or* butter	2 tablespoons
1⅓ cups	whole wheat flour	2 cups
⅔ cup	bread flour	1 cup
2 tablespoons	brown sugar	3 tablespoons
½ teaspoon	salt	¾ teaspoon
¼ teaspoon	ground cinnamon	½ teaspoon
1 teaspoon	active dry yeast *or* bread machine yeast	1 teaspoon

In a medium saucepan combine rhubarb and water. Bring to boiling; reduce heat. Simmer, uncovered, for 5 minutes or till rhubarb is tender. Measure rhubarb-water mixture and add water if necessary to equal 1 cup [1⅓ cups]. Cool slightly. Add ingredients to machine according to manufacturer's directions. Small loaf serves 16.

One teaspoon yeast is recommended by our Test Kitchen for either loaf size (see page 6).

Nutrition information per serving: 69 calories, 2 g protein, 13 g carbohydrate, 1 g fat (0 g saturated), 0 mg cholesterol, 77 mg sodium, 73 mg potassium.

PEAR AND BLUE CHEESE BREAD

1 Pound	Ingredients	1½ Pound
¾ cup	pear nectar *or* apple juice	1 cup plus 2 tablespoons
⅓ cup	crumbled blue cheese	½ cup
1 tablespoon	shortening	2 tablespoons
1⅓ cups	whole wheat flour	2 cups
⅔ cup	bread flour	1 cup
2 teaspoons	brown sugar	1 tablespoon
½ teaspoon	salt	¾ teaspoon
1 teaspoon	active dry yeast *or* bread machine yeast	1 teaspoon

Add ingredients to machine according to manufacturer's directions, adding the cheese with pear nectar. (Use light setting, if available.) Small loaf serves 16.

One teaspoon yeast is recommended by our Test Kitchen for either loaf size (see page 6).

Nutrition information per serving: 81 calories, 3 g protein, 14 g carbohydrate, 2 g fat (1 g saturated), 2 mg cholesterol, 105 mg sodium, 61 mg potassium.

PEACHES AND CREAM PISTACHIO BREAD

1 Pound	Ingredients	1½ Pound
½ cup	dairy sour cream	1 8-ounce carton
⅓ cup	milk	½ cup
1⅓ cups	bread flour	2 cups
⅔ cup	whole wheat flour	1 cup
1 tablespoon	brown sugar	2 tablespoons
½ teaspoon	salt	¾ teaspoon
1 teaspoon	active dry yeast *or* bread machine yeast	1 teaspoon
½ cup	snipped dried peaches	¾ cup
⅓ cup	pistachio nuts	½ cup

Add ingredients to machine according to manufacturer's directions. Small loaf serves 16.
One teaspoon yeast is recommended by our Test Kitchen for either loaf size (see page 6).

Nutrition information per serving: 108 calories, 3 g protein, 17 g carbohydrate, 3 g fat (1 g saturated), 4 mg cholesterol, 74 mg sodium, 133 mg potassium.

SOURDOUGH BREADS

Sourdough Bread 65
Sourdough Rye Bread..66
Dill and Onion Sourdough Bread 67
Pepperoni-Pizza Sourdough Bread 68
Sourdough Wheat Bread.................................... 69
Sourdough Bread with Tarragon and Tomatoes ...70
Sourdough Corn Bread 71
Raisin Sourdough Bread 72
Cranberry-Nut Sourdough Bread 73
Toffee Bread 74

Tips for using Sourdough Starter

For the best results, follow these suggestions before you use the sourdough starter on page 65, or any sourdough starter.

To get the correct amount of starter in your measuring cup, stir the starter thoroughly upon removing it from the refrigerator, then measure it.

The starter should be the consistency of buttermilk or thin pancake batter. If necessary, add water to thin the starter after you have stirred it and before it is measured. The consistency of the starter may change the longer it is stored.

SOURDOUGH BREAD

Sourdough Breads

1 Pound	Ingredients	1½ Pound
¾ cup	**Sourdough Starter (see pages 64–65)**	1¼ cups
¼ cup	**milk *or* water**	2 tablespoons
1 tablespoon	**cooking oil**	1 tablespoon
2 cups	**bread flour**	3 cups
2 teaspoons	**sugar**	1 tablespoon
½ teaspoon	**salt**	¾ teaspoon
1 teaspoon	**active dry yeast *or* bread machine yeast**	1 teaspoon

Add ingredients to machine according to manufacturer's directions. Small loaf serves 16. One teaspoon yeast is recommended by our Test Kitchen for either loaf size (see page 6).
Sourdough Starter: In a large bowl dissolve 1 package *active dry yeast* (not quick-rising yeast) in ½ cup *warm water* (105° to 115°). Stir in 2 cups *warm water,* 2 cups *all-purpose flour,* and 1 tablespoon *sugar or honey.* Beat till smooth. Cover bowl with 100 percent cotton cheesecloth. Let mixture stand at room temperature for 5 to 10 days or till it has a fermented aroma; stir it 2 or 3 times a day. (Fermentation time depends on room temperature; a warmer room hastens fermentation.)

To store, transfer Sourdough Starter to a jar. Cover the jar with 100 percent cotton cheesecloth and refrigerate. *Do not cover the jar tightly with a metal lid.*

To use starter, bring desired amount to room temperature. For each cup of starter used, replenish remaining starter by stirring in ¾ cup *all-purpose flour,* ¾ cup *water,* and 1 teaspoon *sugar or honey.* Cover and let mixture stand at room temperature at least 1 day or till it is bubbly. Refrigerate starter for later use.

If starter isn't used within 10 days, stir in 1 teaspoon *sugar or honey.* Repeat every 10 days unless starter is replenished.

65

Nutrition information per serving: 89 calories, 3 g protein, 17 g carbohydrate, 1 g fat (0 g saturated), 0 mg cholesterol, 68 mg sodium, 30 mg potassium.

SOURDOUGH RYE BREAD

1 Pound	Ingredients	1½ Pound
¾ cup	**Sourdough Starter (see pages 64–65)**	1¼ cups
⅓ cup	**milk *or* water**	¼ cup
1 tablespoon	**cooking oil**	1 tablespoon
1⅓ cups	**bread flour**	2 cups
1 cup	**rye flour**	1½ cups
1 tablespoon	**gluten flour**	2 tablespoons
2 teaspoons	**sugar**	1 tablespoon
½ teaspoon	**salt**	¾ teaspoon
½ teaspoon	**caraway seed**	1 teaspoon
1 teaspoon	**active dry yeast *or* bread machine yeast**	1 teaspoon

Add ingredients to machine according to manufacturer's directions. Small loaf serves 16. One teaspoon yeast is recommended by our Test Kitchen for either loaf size (see page 6).

Nutrition information per serving: 94 calories, 3 g protein, 18 g carbohydrate, 1 g fat (0 g saturated), 0 mg cholesterol, 70 mg sodium, 47 mg potassium.

DILL AND ONION SOURDOUGH BREAD

1 Pound	Ingredients	1½ Pound
⅔ cup	chopped onion	1 cup
1 clove	garlic, minced	1 clove
1 tablespoon	olive oil *or* cooking oil	2 tablespoons
¾ cup	Sourdough Starter (see pages 64–65)	1¼ cups
¼ cup	milk *or* water	2 tablespoons
2 cups	bread flour	3 cups
2 teaspoons	sugar	1 tablespoon
½ teaspoon	salt	¾ teaspoon
½ teaspoon	dried dillweed	¾ teaspoon
1 teaspoon	active dry yeast *or* bread machine yeast	1 teaspoon

In a medium skillet cook onion and garlic in hot oil till onion is tender, stirring occasionally. Cool slightly. Add ingredients to machine according to manufacturer's directions. Small loaf serves 16.

One teaspoon yeast is recommended by our Test Kitchen for either loaf size (see page 6).

Nutrition information per serving: 94 calories, 3 g protein, 18 g carbohydrate, 1 g fat (0 g saturated), 0 mg cholesterol, 70 mg sodium, 47 mg potassium.

Pepperoni-Pizza Sourdough Bread

1 Pound	Ingredients	1½ Pound
¾ cup	**Sourdough Starter (see pages 64–65)**	1¼ cups
¼ cup	**milk *or* water**	2 tablespoons
2 tablespoons	**tomato paste**	3 tablespoons
1 tablespoon	**cooking oil**	1 tablespoon
2 cups	**bread flour**	3 cups
½ cup (2 ounces)	**shredded mozzarella cheese**	¾ cup (3 ounces)
⅓ cup	**finely chopped pepperoni**	½ cup
2 teaspoons	**sugar**	1 tablespoon
½ teaspoon	**salt**	¾ teaspoon
½ teaspoon	**dried oregano, crushed**	¾ tespoon
1 teaspoon	**active dry yeast *or* bread machine yeast**	1 teaspoon

Add ingredients to machine according to manufacturer's directions. Small loaf serves 16. One teaspoon yeast is recommended by our Test Kitchen for either loaf size (see page 6).

Nutrition information per serving: 115 calories, 4 g protein, 17 g carbohydrate, 3 g fat (1 g saturated), 4 mg cholesterol, 141 mg sodium, 67 mg potassium.

SOURDOUGH WHEAT BREAD

1 Pound	Ingredients	1½ Pound
¾ cup	**Sourdough Starter (see pages 64–65)**	1¼ cups
¼ cup	milk *or* water	2 tablespoons
1 tablespoon	cooking oil	1 tablespoon
1⅓ cups	whole wheat flour	2 cups
⅔ cup	bread flour	1 cup
3 tablespoons	toasted wheat germ	¼ cup
2 teaspoons	brown sugar	1 tablespoon
½ teaspoon	salt	¾ teaspoon
1 teaspoon	**active dry yeast *or* bread machine yeast**	1 teaspoon

Add ingredients to machine according to manufacturer's directions. Small loaf serves 12. One teaspoon yeast is recommended by our Test Kitchen for either loaf size (see page 6).

Nutrition information per serving: 118 calories, 4 g protein, 22 g carbohydrate, 2 g fat (0 g saturated), 0 mg cholesterol, 93 mg sodium, 104 mg potassium.

SOURDOUGH BREAD WITH TARRAGON AND TOMATOES

1 Pound	Ingredients	1½ Pound
¾ cup	Sourdough Starter (see pages 64–65)	1¼ cups
¼ cup	milk *or* water	2 tablespoons
1 tablespoon	cooking oil	1 tablespoon
2 cups	bread flour	3 cups
¼ cup	drained and snipped dried tomatoes packed in oil	⅓ cup
2 teaspoons	sugar	1 tablespoon
½ teaspoon	salt	¾ teaspoon
½ teaspoon	dried tarragon, crushed	¾ teaspoon
1 teaspoon	active dry yeast *or* bread machine yeast	1 teaspoon

Add ingredients to machine according to manufacturer's directions, adding the tomatoes with the milk or water. Small loaf serves 16.

One teaspoon yeast is recommended by our Test Kitchen for either loaf size (see page 6).

Nutrition information per serving: 94 calories, 3 g protein, 17 g carbohydrate, 1 g fat (0 g saturated), 0 mg cholesterol, 74 mg sodium, 62 mg potassium.

Sourdough Corn Bread

1 Pound	Ingredients	1½ Pound
¾ cup	Sourdough Starter (see pages 64–65)	1¼ cups
¼ cup	milk *or* water	2 tablespoons
1 tablespoon	cooking oil	1 tablespoon
1¾ cups	bread flour	2⅔ cups
½ cup	canned whole kernel corn, drained	¾ cup
⅓ cup	cornmeal	½ cup
2 teaspoons	sugar	1 tablespoon
½ teaspoon	salt	¾ teaspoon
1 teaspoon	active dry yeast *or* bread machine yeast	1 teaspoon

Add ingredients to machine according to manufacturer's directions, adding the corn with the flour. Small loaf serves 16.

One teaspoon yeast is recommended by our Test Kitchen for either loaf size (see page 6).

Nutrition information per serving: 99 calories, 3 g protein, 19 g carbohydrate, 1 g fat (0 g saturated), 0 mg cholesterol, 87 mg sodium, 49 mg potassium.

Raisin Sourdough Bread

1 Pound	Ingredients	1½ Pound
¾ cup	Sourdough Starter (see pages 64–65)	1¼ cups
¼ cup	milk *or* water	2 tablespoons
1 tablespoon	margarine *or* butter	1 tablespoon
2 cups	bread flour	3 cups
1 tablespoon	brown sugar	2 tablespoons
¾ teaspoon	ground cinnamon	1 teaspoon
½ teaspoon	salt	¾ teaspoon
⅛ teaspoon	ground nutmeg	¼ teaspoon
1 teaspoon	active dry yeast *or* bread machine yeast	1 teaspoon
½ cup	raisins	¾ cup
	Melted margarine *or* butter	
½ teaspoon	sugar	½ teaspoon
⅛ teaspoon	ground cinnamon	⅛ teaspoon

Add the first 10 ingredients to machine according to manufacturer's directions. After removing baked bread from machine, brush top of loaf with melted margarine or butter. Stir together sugar and the ⅛ teaspoon cinnamon and sprinkle over top of loaf. Small loaf serves 16.

One teaspoon yeast is recommended by our Test Kitchen for either loaf size (see page 6).

Nutrition information per serving: 108 calories, 3 g protein, 21 g carbohydrate, 1 g fat (0 g saturated), 0 mg cholesterol, 81 mg sodium, 73 mg potassium.

CRANBERRY-NUT SOURDOUGH BREAD

1 Pound	Ingredients	1½ Pound
¾ cup	Sourdough Starter (see pages 64–65)	1¼ cups
1½ teaspoons	finely shredded orange peel	2 teaspoons
¼ cup	orange juice *or* water	2 tablespoons
1 tablespoon	cooking oil	1 tablespoon
2 cups	bread flour	3 cups
⅓ cup	snipped dried cranberries	½ cup
⅓ cup	toasted chopped almonds *or* walnuts	½ cup
2 teaspoons	sugar	1 tablespoon
½ teaspoon	salt	¾ teaspoon
1 teaspoon	active dry yeast *or* bread machine yeast	1 teaspoon
	Powdered Sugar Glaze	
	Toasted sliced almonds	

Add the first 10 ingredients to machine according to manufacturer's directions. When bread is cool, drizzle top of loaf with Powdered Sugar Glaze and sprinkle with sliced almonds. Small loaf serves 16.

One teaspoon yeast is recommended by our Test Kitchen for either loaf size (see page 6).

Powdered Sugar Glaze: In a bowl stir together ½ cup sifted *powdered sugar*, ½ teaspoon *vanilla*, and enough *milk* (2 to 3 teaspoons) to make a glaze of drizzling consistency.

Nutrition information per serving: 127 calories, 3 g protein, 23 g carbohydrate, 3 g fat (0 g saturated), 0 mg cholesterol, 69 mg sodium, 58 mg potassium.

TOFFEE BREAD

1 Pound	Ingredients	1½ Pound
1½ teaspoons	**instant coffee crystals**	2 teaspoons
¼ cup	**milk *or* water**	2 tablespoons
¾ cup	**Sourdough Starter (see pages 64–65)**	1¼ cups
1 tablespoon	**margarine *or* butter**	2 tablespoons
2 cups	**bread flour**	3 cups
1 tablespoon	**sugar**	4 teaspoons
½ teaspoon	**salt**	1 teaspoon
1 teaspoon	**active dry yeast *or* bread machine yeast**	1 teaspoon
⅓ cup	**almond brickle pieces**	½ cup

Dissolve coffee crystals in the milk or water. Add ingredients to machine according to manufacturer's directions. (Use light setting, if available.) Small loaf serves 16.

One teaspoon yeast is recommended by our Test Kitchen for either loaf size (see page 6).

Nutrition information per serving: 110 calories, 3 g protein, 19 g carbohydrate, 2 g fat (0 g saturated), 2 mg cholesterol, 98 mg sodium, 41 mg potassium.

RYE BREADS

Rye Bread 76
Swiss Rye Bread 77
Dill and Rye Beer Bread 78
Tomato Rye Bread 79
Yogurt Rye Bread.. 80
Reuben Rye Bread 81
Mustard Rye Bread 82
Orange and Spice Rye Bread 83
Pumpernickel-Prune Bread........................... 84
Fruit and Nut Bread 85

Rye Bread

1 Pound	Ingredients	1½ Pound
¾ cup	water	1¼ cups
1 tablespoon	shortening	1 tablespoon
1⅓ cups	bread flour	2 cups
1 cup	rye flour	1½ cups
1 tablespoon	gluten flour	2 tablespoons
2 teaspoons	brown sugar	1 tablespoon
½ teaspoon	caraway seed	1 teaspoon
½ teaspoon	salt	¾ teaspoon
1 teaspoon	active dry yeast *or* bread machine yeast	1 teaspoon

Add ingredients to machine according to manufacturer's directions. Small loaf serves 16. One teaspoon yeast is recommended by our Test Kitchen for either loaf size (see page 6).

Nutrition information per serving: 75 calories, 2 g protein, 14 g carbohydrate, 1 g fat (0 g saturated), 0 mg cholesterol, 68 mg sodium, 34 mg potassium.

SWISS RYE BREAD

1 Pound	Ingredients	1½ Pound
¾ cup plus 2 tablespoons	water	1⅓ cups
1 tablespoon	shortening	1 tablespoon
1⅓ cups	bread flour	2 cups
1 cup	rye flour	1½ cups
½ cup (2 ounces)	shredded Swiss *or* cheddar cheese	¾ cup (3 ounces)
1 tablespoon	gluten flour	2 tablespoons
2 teaspoons	brown sugar	1 tablespoon
½ teaspoon	caraway seed	1 teaspoon
½ teaspoon	salt	¾ teaspoon
1 teaspoon	active dry yeast *or* bread machine yeast	1 teaspoon

Add ingredients to machine according to manufacturer's directions. Small loaf serves 16. One teaspoon yeast is recommended by our Test Kitchen for either loaf size (see page 6).

Nutrition information per serving: 88 calories, 3 g protein, 14 g carbohydrate, 2 g fat (1 g saturated), 3 mg cholesterol, 77 mg sodium, 37 mg potassium.

DILL AND RYE BEER BREAD

1 Pound	Ingredients	1½ Pound
¾ cup	beer	1¼ cups
1 tablespoon	shortening	1 tablespoon
1⅓ cups	bread flour	2 cups
1 cup	rye flour	1½ cups
1 tablespoon	gluten flour	2 tablespoons
2 teaspoons	brown sugar	1 tablespoon
¾ teaspoon	dried dillweed	1 teaspoon
½ teaspoon	caraway seed	1 teaspoon
½ teaspoon	salt	¾ teaspoon
1 teaspoon	active dry yeast *or* bread machine yeast	1 teaspoon

Add ingredients to machine according to manufacturer's directions. Small loaf serves 16. One teaspoon yeast is recommended by our Test Kitchen for either loaf size (see page 6).

Nutrition information per serving: 79 calories, 2 g protein, 14 g carbohydrate, 1 g fat (0 g saturated), 0 mg cholesterol, 68 mg sodium, 38 mg potassium.

TOMATO RYE BREAD

1 Pound	Ingredients	1½ Pound
¾ cup	water	1¼ cups plus 2 tablespoons
2 tablespoons	tomato paste	3 tablespoons
1 tablespoon	shortening	1 tablespoon
1⅓ cups	bread flour	2 cups
1 cup	rye flour	1½ cups
1 tablespoon	gluten flour	2 tablespoons
2 teaspoons	brown sugar	1 tablespoon
½ teaspoon	caraway seed	1 teaspoon
½ teaspoon	salt	¾ teaspoon
½ teaspoon	dried oregano, crushed	¾ teaspoon
¼ teaspoon	dried basil, crushed	½ teaspoon
1 teaspoon	active dry yeast *or* bread machine yeast	1 teaspoon

Add ingredients to machine according to manufacturer's directions. Small loaf serves 16. One teaspoon yeast is recommended by our Test Kitchen for either loaf size (see page 6).

Nutrition information per serving: 81 calories, 2 g protein, 16 g carbohydrate, 1 g fat (0 g saturated), 0 mg cholesterol, 84 mg sodium, 57 mg potassium.

YOGURT RYE BREAD

1 Pound	Ingredients	1½ Pound
½ cup	**plain yogurt**	1 8-ounce carton
⅓ cup	**water**	½ cup
1 tablespoon	**shortening**	1 tablespoon
1⅓ cups	**bread flour**	2 cups
1 cup	**rye flour**	1½ cups
1 tablespoon	**gluten flour**	2 tablespoons
2 teaspoons	**brown sugar**	1 tablespoon
½ teaspoon	**caraway seed**	1 teaspoon
½ teaspoon	**salt**	¾ teaspoon
1 teaspoon	**active dry yeast *or* bread machine yeast**	1 teaspoon

Add ingredients to machine according to manufacturer's directions. Small loaf serves 16. One teaspoon yeast is recommended by our Test Kitchen for either loaf size (see page 6).

Nutrition information per serving: 79 calories, 2 g protein, 15 g carbohydrate, 1 g fat (0 g saturated), 0 mg cholesterol, 72 mg sodium, 50 mg potassium.

REUBEN RYE BREAD

1 Pound	Ingredients	1½ Pound
¾ cup	water	1 cup
⅓ cup	snipped sauerkraut, rinsed and well drained	½ cup
1 tablespoon	shortening	1 tablespoon
1⅔ cups	bread flour	2 cups
1 cup	rye flour	1½ cups
1 tablespoon	gluten flour	2 tablespoons
2 teaspoons	brown sugar	1 tablespoon
½ teaspoon	caraway seed	1 teaspoon
½ teaspoon	salt	¾ teaspoon
1 teaspoon	active dry yeast *or* bread machine yeast	1 teaspoon
½ cup	chopped corned beef	¾ cup

Add ingredients to machine according to manufacturer's directions, adding the sauerkraut with the water. If desired, to serve, toast slices of bread and top them with Thousand Island dressing and slices of melted Swiss cheese. Store leftover bread in the refrigerator. Small loaf serves 16.

One teaspoon yeast is recommended by our Test Kitchen for either loaf size (see page 6).

Nutrition information per serving: 79 calories, 3 g protein, 14 g carbohydrate, 1 g fat (0 g saturated), 3 mg cholesterol, 142 mg sodium, 40 mg potassium.

MUSTARD RYE BREAD

1 Pound	Ingredients	1½ Pound
¾ cup	water	1¼ cups
3 tablespoons	Dijon-style *or* brown mustard	¼ cup
1 tablespoon	shortening	1 tablespoon
1⅓ cups	bread flour	2 cups
1 cup	rye flour	1½ cups
1 tablespoon	gluten flour	2 tablespoons
2 teaspoons	brown sugar	1 tablespoon
½ teaspoon	caraway seed	1 teaspoon
½ teaspoon	salt	¾ teaspoon
1 teaspoon	active dry yeast *or* bread machine yeast	1 teaspoon

Add ingredients to machine according to manufacturer's directions. Small loaf serves 16. One teaspoon yeast is recommended by our Test Kitchen for either loaf size (see page 6).

Nutrition information per serving: 78 calories, 3 g protein, 14 g carbohydrate, 1 g fat (0 g saturated), 0 mg cholesterol, 139 mg sodium, 38 mg potassium.

ORANGE AND SPICE RYE BREAD

1 Pound	Ingredients	1½ Pound
1 teaspoon	finely shredded orange peel	1½ teaspoons
½ cup	orange juice *or* water	¾ cup
¼ cup	water	½ cup
1 tablespoon	shortening	1 tablespoon
1⅓ cups	bread flour	2 cups
1 cup	rye flour	1½ cups
1 tablespoon	gluten flour	2 tablespoons
1 tablespoon	brown sugar	4 teaspoons
¾ teaspoon	ground cinnamon	1 teaspoon
½ teaspoon	salt	¾ teaspoon
1 teaspoon	active dry yeast *or* bread machine yeast	1 teaspoon

Add ingredients to machine according to manufacturer's directions. Small loaf serves 16.
One teaspoon yeast is recommended by our Test Kitchen for either loaf size (see page 6).

Nutrition information per serving: 79 calories, 2 g protein, 15 g carbohydrate, 1 g fat (0 g saturated), 0 mg cholesterol, 68 mg sodium, 48 mg potassium.

PUMPERNICKEL-PRUNE BREAD

1 Pound	Ingredients	1½ Pound
¾ cup	water	1¼ cups
1 tablespoon	shortening	1 tablespoon
1⅓ cups	bread flour	2 cups
½ cup	rye flour	¾ cup
⅓ cup	whole wheat flour	½ cup
2 tablespoons	cornmeal	¼ cup
1 tablespoon	gluten flour	2 tablespoons
2 teaspoons	brown sugar	1 tablespoon
½ teaspoon	salt	¾ teaspoon
1 teaspoon	active dry yeast *or* bread machine yeast	1 teaspoon
¼ cup	chopped pitted prunes	½ cup

Add ingredients to machine according to manufacturer's directions. Small loaf serves 16. One teaspoon yeast is recommended by our Test Kitchen for either loaf size (see page 6).

Nutrition information per serving: 81 calories, 2 g protein, 16 g carbohydrate, 1 g fat (0 g saturated), 0 mg cholesterol, 68 mg sodium, 56 mg potassium.

FRUIT AND NUT BREAD

1 Pound	Ingredients	1½ Pound
¾ cup plus 2 tablespoons	water	1⅓ cups
1 tablespoon	margarine *or* butter	1 tablespoon
1⅓ cups	bread flour	2 cups
1 cup	rye flour	1½ cups
1 tablespoon	gluten flour	2 tablespoons
2 teaspoons	brown sugar	2 tablespoons
½ teaspoon	caraway seed	1 teaspoon
½ teaspoon	salt	¾ teaspoon
1 teaspoon	active dry yeast *or* bread machine yeast	1 teaspoon
½ cup	mixed dried fruit bits	¾ cup
⅓ cup	toasted chopped walnuts	½ cup

Add ingredients to machine according to manufacturer's directions. Small loaf serves 16.
One teaspoon yeast is recommended by our Test Kitchen for either loaf size (see page 6).

Nutrition information per serving: 95 calories, 3 g protein, 17 g carbohydrate, 2 g fat (0 g saturated), 0 mg cholesterol, 79 mg sodium, 74 mg potassium.

EGG BREADS

Egg Bread.. 87
Chili Cheese Bread 88
Herbed Pumpkin Bread 89
Apricot-Pecan Breakfast Loaf 90
Banana-Walnut Bread 91
Peanut Butter Snack Bread 92
Currant-Nut Coffee Bread 93
Panettone 94
Saffron-Fruit Bread 95
Hawaiian Bread 96
Hazelnut-Amaretto Bread 97
Blueberry-Black Walnut Bread 98
Gingerbread Loaf 99
Chocolate-Cherry Bread 100

EGG BREAD

1 Pound	Ingredients	1½ Pound
⅔ cup	milk	1 cup
1	egg	1
1 tablespoon	margarine *or* butter	1 tablespoon
2 cups	bread flour	3 cups
4 teaspoons	sugar	2 tablespoons
½ teaspoon	salt	¾ teaspoon
1 teaspoon	active dry yeast *or* bread machine yeast	1 teaspoon

Add ingredients to machine according to manufacturer's directions. Small loaf serves 16. One teaspoon yeast is recommended by our Test Kitchen for either loaf size (see page 6).

Nutrition information per serving: 78 calories, 3 g protein, 14 g carbohydrate, 1 g fat (0 g saturated), 10 mg cholesterol, 80 mg sodium, 39 mg potassium.

CHILI CHEESE BREAD

1 Pound	Ingredients	1½ Pound
⅔ cup	milk	1 cup
1	egg	1
2 cups	bread flour	3 cups
½ cup (2 ounces)	diced Monterey Jack cheese with jalapeño peppers	¾ cup (3 ounces)
1 tablespoon	sugar	4 teaspoons
½ teaspoon	salt	¾ teaspoon
⅛ teaspoon	ground red pepper	¼ teaspoon
1 teaspoon	active dry yeast *or* bread machine yeast	1 teaspoon

Add ingredients to machine according to manufacturer's directions. Small loaf serves 16. One teaspoon yeast is recommended by our Test Kitchen for either loaf size (see page 6).

Nutrition information per serving: 88 calories, 4 g protein, 14 g carbohydrate, 2 g fat (1 g saturated), 17 mg cholesterol, 95 mg sodium, 44 mg potassium.

HERBED PUMPKIN BREAD

1 Pound	Ingredients	1½ Pound
½ cup	canned pumpkin	¾ cup
⅓ cup	half-and-half, light cream, *or* milk	½ cup
1	egg	1
1 tablespoon	margarine *or* butter	2 tablespoons
2 cups	bread flour	3 cups
2 tablespoons	brown sugar	3 tablespoons
½ teaspoon	salt	¾ teaspoon
¼ teaspoon	dried basil, crushed	½ teaspoon
⅛ teaspoon	dried rosemary, crushed	¼ teaspoon
1 teaspoon	active dry yeast *or* bread machine yeast	1 teaspoon

Add ingredients to machine according to manufacturer's directions. Small loaf serves 16. One teaspoon yeast is recommended by our Test Kitchen for either loaf size (see page 6).

Nutrition information per serving: 89 calories, 3 g protein, 15 g carbohydrate, 2 g fat (1 g saturated), 15 mg cholesterol, 82 mg sodium, 55 mg potassium.

APRICOT-PECAN BREAKFAST LOAF

1 Pound	Ingredients	1½ Pound
⅔ cup	milk	1 cup
1	egg	1
1 tablespoon	margarine *or* butter	1 tablespoon
2 cups	bread flour	3 cups
½ cup	snipped dried apricots	⅔ cup
3 tablespoons	sugar	¼ cup
3 tablespoons	toasted chopped pecans	¼ cup
½ teaspoon	salt	¾ teaspoon
1 teaspoon	active dry yeast *or* bread machine yeast	1 teaspoon
	Apricot Icing (optional)	

Add the first 9 ingredients to machine according to manufacturer's directions. (Use light setting, if available.) If desired, when bread is cool, drizzle loaf with Apricot Icing. Small loaf serves 16.

One teaspoon yeast is recommended by our Test Kitchen for either loaf size (see page 6).

Apricot Icing: In a small mixing bowl stir together ½ cup sifted *powdered sugar* and enough *apricot nectar* (2 to 3 teaspoons) to make an icing of drizzling consistency.

Nutrition information per serving: 106 calories, 3 g protein, 19 g carbohydrate, 2 g fat (0 g saturated), 13 mg cholesterol, 80 mg sodium, 99 mg potassium.

BANANA-WALNUT BREAD

1 Pound	Ingredients	1½ Pound
½ cup	milk	⅔ cup
⅓ cup	mashed ripe banana	½ cup
1	egg	1
1 tablespoon	margarine *or* butter	2 tablespoons
2 cups	bread flour	3 cups
2 tablespoons	sugar	3 tablespoons
½ teaspoon	salt	¾ teaspoon
⅛ teaspoon	ground cinnamon (optional)	¼ teaspoon
1 teaspoon	active dry yeast *or* bread machine yeast	1 teaspoon
½ cup	toasted chopped walnuts *or* pecans	¾ cup

Add ingredients to machine according to manufacturer's directions, adding the banana with the milk. (Use light setting, if available.) Small loaf serves 16.

One teaspoon yeast is recommended by our Test Kitchen for either loaf size (see page 6).

Nutrition information per serving: 110 calories, 3 g protein, 16 g carbohydrate, 4 g fat (1 g saturated), 14 mg cholesterol, 84 mg sodium, 70 mg potassium.

PEANUT BUTTER SNACK BREAD

1 Pound	Ingredients	1½ Pound
¾ cup	milk	1 cup plus 2 tablespoons
¼ cup	peanut butter	⅓ cup
1	egg	1
2 cups	bread flour	3 cups
4 teaspoons	sugar	2 tablespoons
½ teaspoon	salt	¾ teaspoon
1 teaspoon	active dry yeast *or* bread machine yeast	1 teaspoon
½ cup	chopped peanuts	¾ cup

Add ingredients to machine according to manufacturer's directions. Small loaf serves 16. One teaspoon yeast is recommended by our Test Kitchen for either loaf size (see page 6).

Nutrition information per serving: 126 calories, 5 g protein, 16 g carbohydrate, 5 g fat (1 g saturated), 14 mg cholesterol, 96 mg sodium, 102 mg potassium.

CURRANT-NUT COFFEE BREAD

1 Pound	Ingredients	1½ Pound
1 teaspoon	instant coffee crystals	1½ teaspoons
⅔ cup	water	1 cup
1	egg	1
1 tablespoon	margarine *or* butter	1 tablespoon
2 cups	bread flour	3 cups
2 tablespoons	brown sugar	3 tablespoons
½ teaspoon	salt	¾ teaspoon
¾ teaspoon	active dry yeast *or* bread machine yeast	1 teaspoon
⅓ cup	dried currants *or* dried tart red cherries	½ cup
¼ cup	toasted chopped almonds *or* pecans	⅓ cup

Dissolve coffee crystals in water. Add ingredients to machine according to manufacturer's directions. (Use light setting, if available.) Small loaf serves 16.

One teaspoon yeast is recommended by our Test Kitchen for either loaf size (see page 6).

Nutrition information per serving: 101 calories, 3 g protein, 17 g carbohydrate, 2 g fat (0 g saturated), 13 mg cholesterol, 81 mg sodium, 77 mg potassium.

PANETTONE BREAD

1 Pound	Ingredients	1½ Pound
⅔ cup	milk	¾ cup
1	egg	1
1 tablespoon	margarine *or* butter	3 tablespoons
2 cups	bread flour	3 cups
1 tablespoon	honey	2 tablespoons
1 teaspoon	aniseed, crushed	1½ teaspoons
½ teaspoon	salt	¾ teaspoon
1 teaspoon	active dry yeast *or* bread machine yeast	1 teaspoon
¼ cup	light raisins	⅓ cup
¼ cup	dried currants	⅓ cup
¼ cup	chopped candied citron	⅓ cup

Add ingredients to machine according to manufacturer's directions. (Use light setting, if available.) Small loaf serves 16.

One teaspoon yeast is recommended by our Test Kitchen for either loaf size (see page 6).

Nutrition information per serving: 103 calories, 3 g protein, 19 g carbohydrate, 2 g fat (0 g saturated), 14 mg cholesterol, 85 mg sodium, 83 mg potassium.

SAFFRON-FRUIT BREAD

1 Pound	Ingredients	1½ Pound
⅔ cup	milk	1 cup
1	egg	1
2 tablespoons	margarine *or* butter	3 tablespoons
2 cups	bread flour	3 cups
2 tablespoons	sugar	3 tablespoons
1 teaspoon	finely shredded orange peel	1½ teaspoons
½ teaspoon	salt	¾ teaspoon
Pinch	thread saffron, crushed, *or* dash ground saffron	Pinch
¾ teaspoon	active dry yeast *or* bread machine yeast	1 teaspoon
¼ cup	light raisins	⅓ cup
¼ cup	dark raisins	⅓ cup

Add ingredients to machine according to manufacturer's directions. Small loaf serves 16. One teaspoon yeast is recommended by our Test Kitchen for either loaf size (see page 6).

Nutrition information per serving: 105 calories, 3 g protein, 18 g carbohydrate, 2 g fat (1 g saturated), 14 mg cholesterol, 93 mg sodium, 77 mg potassium.

HAWAIIAN BREAD

1 Pound	Ingredients	1½ Pound
⅓ cup	water	½ cup
⅓ cup	pineapple juice	½ cup
1	egg	1
1 tablespoon	margarine *or* butter	2 tablespoons
2 cups	bread flour	3 cups
2 tablespoons	sugar	3 tablespoons
½ teaspoon	salt	¾ teaspoon
1 teaspoon	active dry yeast *or* bread machine yeast	1 teaspoon
½ cup	chopped macadamia nuts *or* almonds	¾ cup
⅓ cup	coconut	½ cup

Add ingredients to machine according to manufacturer's directions. Small loaf serves 16. One teaspoon yeast is recommended by our Test Kitchen for either loaf size (see page 6).

Nutrition information per serving: 119 calories, 3 g protein, 16 g carbohydrate, 5 g fat (1 g saturated), 13 mg cholesterol, 80 mg sodium, 51 mg potassium.

HAZELNUT-AMARETTO LOAF

1 Pound	Ingredients	1½ Pound
⅔ cup	milk	1 cup
1	egg	1
4 teaspoons	amaretto *or* hazelnut liqueur	2 tablespoons
2 tablespoons	margarine *or* butter	3 tablespoons
2 cups	bread flour	3 cups
2 tablespoons	sugar	3 tablespoons
½ teaspoon	salt	¾ teaspoon
¾ teaspoon	active dry yeast *or* bread machine yeast	1 teaspoon
½ cup	toasted chopped hazelnuts	¾ cup
	Amaretto Glaze	

Add the first 9 ingredients to machine according to manufacturer's directions. When bread is cool, drizzle bread with Amaretto Glaze. Small loaf serves 16.
One teaspoon yeast is recommended by our Test Kitchen for either loaf size (see page 6).

Amaretto Glaze: In a small mixing bowl stir together ½ cup sifted *powdered sugar* and 1 tablespoon *Amaretteo or hazelnut liqueur.* If necessary, add 1 to 2 teaspoons *milk* to make a glaze of drizzling consistency.

Nutrition information per serving: 130 calories, 3 g protein, 19 g carbohydrate, 4 g fat (1 g saturated), 14 mg cholesterol, 93 mg sodium, 58 mg potassium.

BLUEBERRY-BLACK WALNUT BREAD

1 Pound	Ingredients	1½ Pound
⅓ cup	vanilla yogurt	½ cup
⅓ cup	milk	½ cup
1	egg	1
1 tablespoon	margarine *or* butter	2 tablespoons
2 cups	bread flour	3 cups
½ teaspoon	salt	¾ teaspoon
1 teaspoon	active dry yeast *or* bread machine yeast	1 teaspoon
¼ cup	dried blueberries *or*	⅓ cup
	snipped dried tart red cherries	
¼ cup	chopped black walnuts	⅓ cup

Add ingredients to machine according to manufacturer's directions. Small loaf serves 16. One teaspoon yeast is recommended by our Test Kitchen for either loaf size (see page 6).

Nutrition information per serving: 106 calories, 4 g protein, 17 g carbohydrate, 3 g fat (0 g saturated), 14 mg cholesterol, 87 mg sodium, 60 mg potassium.

GINGERBREAD LOAF

1 Pound	Ingredients	1½ Pound
½ cup	milk	¾ cup
3 tablespoons	light molasses	¼ cup
1	egg	1
2 tablespoons	margarine *or* butter	3 tablespoons
2 1/4 cups	bread flour	3⅓ cups
2 teaspoons	brown sugar	1 tablespoon
½ teaspoon	salt	¾ teaspoon
½ teaspoon	ground cinnamon	¾ teaspoon
½ teaspoon	ground ginger	¾ teaspoon
1 teaspoon	active dry yeast *or* bread machine yeast	1 teaspoon
	Lemon Icing (optional)	

Add the first 10 ingredients to machine according to manufacturer's directions. (Use light setting, if available.) If desired, when bread is cool, drizzle bread with Lemon Icing. Small loaf serves 16.

One teaspoon yeast is recommended by our Test Kitchen for either loaf size (see page 6).

Lemon Icing: In a small mixing bowl stir together ½ cup sifted *powdered sugar,* ¼ teaspoon *vanilla,* 1 teaspoon *lemon juice* and enough *milk* (1 to 3 teaspoons) to make an icing of drizzling consistency.

Nutrition information per serving: 103 calories, 3 g protein, 18 g carbohydrate, 2 g fat (1 g saturated), 14 mg cholesterol, 92 mg sodium, 77 mg potassium.

CHOCOLATE-CHERRY BREAD

1 Pound	Ingredients	1½ Pound
⅔ cup	milk	1 cup
1	egg	1
2 tablespoons	margarine *or* butter	3 tablespoons
2 cups	bread flour	3 cups
¼ cup	sugar	⅓ cup
¼ cup	unsweetened cocoa powder	⅓ cup
½ teaspoon	salt	¾ teaspoon
¾ teaspoon	active dry yeast *or* bread machine yeast	1 teaspoon
½ cup	snipped dried tart red cherries	⅔ cup
¼ cup	chopped pecans	⅓ cup

Add ingredients to machine according to manufacturer's directions. Small loaf serves 16. One teaspoon yeast is recommended by our Test Kitchen for either loaf size (see page 6).

Nutrition information per serving: 122 calories, 3 g protein, 20 g carbohydrate, 3 g fat (1 g saturated), 14 mg cholesterol, 94 mg sodium, 116 mg potassium.

SHAPED BREADS, ROLLS, AND COFFEE CAKES

Pizza Dough..102
Chicken and Cheese Bread....................104
French Bread...106
Cracked Wheat Italian Bread 108
Golden Onion Bread 110
Pepper and Parmesan Bread.................112
Sour Cream-Wheat Dinner Rolls...........114
Bran-Bulgur Butterhorns 116
Cheddar Cheese Bows 118
Oatmeal-Cherry Rolls 120
Whole Wheat English Muffins..............122
Coffee and Cream Rolls........................124
Maple-Oat Breakfast Buns 126
Almond Loaf 128
Swirled Cinnamon-Apple Bread............130
Apricot-and-Chocolate-Filled
Ladder Loaves......................................132
Spiced Chocolate and Rye Coffee Cake..134
Apricot-Almond Wreaths 136
Mincemeat Coffee Bread......................138
Cherry-Almond Coffee Bread...............140
Peanut Butter-Chocolate Bubble Ring...142

PIZZA DOUGH

1 Pound	Ingredients	1½ Pound
⅔ cup	water	1 cup
4 teaspoons	cooking oil	2 tablespoons
2 cups	bread flour	3 cups
½ teaspoon	salt	¾ teaspoon
1 teaspoon	active dry yeast *or* bread machine yeast	1 teaspoon
	Cornmeal (optional)	

Add the frist 5 ingredients to machine according to manufacturer's directions. Select dough setting.

When cycle is complete, remove dough from machine. [Divide dough in half. If desired, freeze half to use another time. Wrap it in plastic wrap and transfer to a freezer bag. Seal, label, and freeze for up to 3 months. To thaw, let dough stand at room temperature about 2½ hours or till thawed. *Or,* thaw overnight in the refrigerator.]

For each thin pizza, grease a 12-inch pizza pan or large baking sheet. If desired, sprinkle with cornmeal. On a lightly floured surface, roll [half of] the dough into a 13-inch circle. Transfer to pan or baking sheet. Do not let dough rise. Bake in a 425° oven about 12 minutes or till browned. Top with pizza sauce and toppings of your choice. Bake 10 to 15 minutes more or till bubbly.

For each pan pizza, grease a 9x9x2-inch baking pan. If desired, sprinkle with cornmeal. With greased fingers, pat [half of] the dough into the bottom and halfway up the sides of prepared pan. Cover and let rise in a warm place till nearly double (30 to 45 minutes). Bake in a 375° oven for 20 to 25 minutes or till lightly browned. Top with pizza sauce and toppings of your choice. Bake 15 to 20 minutes more or till bubbly. Makes 1 crust [2 crusts] of 4 servings [each].

One teaspoon yeast is recommended by our Test Kitchen for either size (see page 6).

Nutrition information per serving: 290 calories, 9 g protein, 50 g carbohydrate, 6 g fat (1 g saturated), 0 mg cholesterol, 269 mg sodium, 86 mg potassium.

CHICKEN AND CHEESE BREAD

1 Pound	Ingredients	1½ Pounds
¾ cup	water	-
2½ cups	bread flour	-
1 tablespoon	sugar	-
½ teaspoon	salt	-
1 teaspoon	active dry yeast *or* bread machine yeast	-
2 cups	chopped cooked chicken	-
1½ cups	shredded cheddar, Swiss *or* provolone cheese(6 ounces)	-
1 10-ounce package	frozen chopped spinach, thawed and well drained	-
¼ cup	grated Parmesan cheese	-
¼ cup	finely chopped onion	-
¼ teaspoon	salt	-
1	beaten egg white	-
1 tablespoon	water	-
2 teaspoons	sesame seed	-

Add the first 5 ingredients to the machine according to manufacturer's directions. Select dough cycle.

Meanwhile, for filling, in a large mixing bowl stir together chicken; cheddar, Swiss, or provolone cheese; spinach; Parmesan cheese; onion; and ¼ teaspoon salt.

When cycle is complete, remove dough from machine. Cover and let rest 10 minutes. On a lightly floured surface, roll dough into a 16x10-inch rectangle. Spread the filling lengthwise down the center third of the dough rectangle. Bring long edges together over filling. Moisten and pinch to seal edges and ends.

Carefully lift and place seam side down on a greased baking sheet. Combine egg white and water; brush over top of loaf. Sprinkle with sesame seed. (Do not let bread rise.)

Bake in a 375° oven for 40 minutes or till bread sounds hollow when tapped. If necessary, cover with foil during the last 10 minutes of baking to prevent overbrowning. Remove from baking sheet; cool slightly. Serve warm or chilled. Makes 8 main-dish servings.

One teaspoon yeast is recommended by our Test Kitchen (see page 6).

Nutrition information per serving: 353 calories, 25 g protein, 36 g carbohydrate, 12 g fat (6 g saturated), 60 mg cholesterol, 463 mg sodium, 293 mg potassium.

FRENCH BREAD

1 Pound	Ingredients	1½ Pound
¾ cup	water	1¼ cups
2½ cups	bread flour	3¾ cups
½ teaspoon	salt	¾ teaspoon
1 teaspoon	active dry yeast *or* bread machine yeast	1 teaspoon
	Cornmeal	
1	slightly beaten egg white	1
1 tablespoon	water	1 tablespoon

Add the first 4 ingredients to the machine according to manufacturer's directions. Select dough setting.

When cycle is complete, remove dough from machine. Let rest 10 minutes. On a lightly floured surface, roll dough into a 15x10-inch rectangle. [Divide 1½ pound recipe in half and roll each half into a 10x8-inch rectangle.] Roll up jelly-roll style, starting from one of the long sides; seal well. Pinch and pull ends to taper.

Place seam side down on a greased baking sheet sprinkled with cornmeal. Combine egg white and water; brush some of it over top of loaf. Cover and let rise till nearly double (35 to 45 minutes). With a very sharp knife, make 3 or 4 diagonal cuts about ¼ inch deep across the top of loaf.

Bake in a 375° oven for 20 minutes. Brush again with remaining egg white and water mixture. Continue baking for 12 to 15 minutes or till bread sounds hollow when tapped with your fingers. Remove from baking sheet; cool. Makes 10 [15] servings.

One teaspoon yeast is recommended by our Test Kitchen for either loaf size (see page 6).

Nutrition information per serving: 81 calories, 3 g protein, 16 g carbohydrate, 0 g fat (0 g saturated), 0 mg cholesterol, 71 mg sodium, 30 mg potassium.

CRACKED WHEAT ITALIAN BREAD

1 Pound	Ingredients	1½ Pound
¾ cup	water	1¼ cups
2 teaspoons	molasses	1 tablespoon
1½ teaspoons	shortening *or* cooking oil	2 teaspoons
2 cups	bread flour	3 cups
½ cup	cracked wheat	¾ cup
½ teaspoon	salt	¾ teaspoon
1 teaspoon	active dry yeast *or* bread machine yeast	1 teaspoon
	Cornmeal	
	Milk	

Add the first 7 ingredients to machine according to manufacturer's directions. Select dough cycle.

When cycle is complete, remove dough from machine. Cover and let rest for 10 minutes. On a lightly floured surface, roll dough into a 15x10-inch rectangle. [For 1½ pound recipe, divide dough in half. Roll each half into a 10x8-inch rectangle.] Roll up jelly-roll style, starting from one of the long sides; seal well. Pinch and pull ends to taper.

Place seam side down on a greased baking sheet sprinkled with cornmeal. Cover and let rise till nearly double (about 45 minutes). With a very sharp knife, make 3 or 4 diagonal cuts about ¼ inch deep across the top of loaf. Brush loaf with milk.

Bake in a 375° oven for 30 to 35 minutes or till bread sounds hollow when tapped with your fingers. Remove from baking sheet; cool. Makes 16 [24] servings.

One teaspoon yeast is recommended by our Test Kitchen for either loaf size (see page 6).

Individual Loaves: Remove dough from machine. Divide into fourths [sixths]. Let rest 10 minutes. Roll each portion into a 8x6-inch rectangle. Roll up from one of the long sides; seal well. Pinch and pull ends to taper. Continue as directed above.

Nutrition information per serving: 80 calories, 3 g protein, 16 g carbohydrate, 1 g fat (0 g saturated), 0 mg cholesterol, 68 mg sodium, 42 mg potassium.

GOLDEN ONION BREAD

1 Pound	Ingredients	1½ Pound
⅔ cup	milk	1 cup
1	egg	1
1 tablespoon	margarine *or* butter	1 tablespoon
2¼ cups	bread flour	3⅓ cups
4 teaspoons	sugar	2 tablespoons
½ teaspoon	salt	¾ teaspoon
1 teaspoon	active dry yeast *or* bread machine yeast	1 teaspoon
1¼ cups	chopped onion	1½ cups
¾ teaspoon	dried basil, crushed	1 teaspoon
¾ teaspoon	paprika	1 teaspoon
2 tablespoons	margarine *or* butter	2 tablespoons
1	egg yolk	1
1 tablespoon	water	1 tablespoon

Add the first 7 ingredients to machine according to manufacturer's directions. Select dough cycle.

When cycle is complete, remove dough from machine. Cover and let rest 10 minutes.

Meanwhile, in a large skillet cook onion, basil, and paprika in the 2 tablespoons margarine or butter till onion is tender but not brown. Cool slightly.

On a lightly floured surface, roll dough into a 12x9-inch [15x9-inch] rectangle. Cut into three 12x3-inch [15x3-inch] strips. Spread each strip with a third of the onion mixture to within ½ inch of each edge. Combine egg yolk and water; brush some of the mixture around edges of each dough strip. Fold each strip in half lengthwise; seal the side and ends.

Place strips seam side down, side by side, on a greased baking sheet. Loosely braid strips together, beginning in the middle and working toward ends. Pinch ends together and tuck under braid. Cover and let rise in a warm place till nearly double (about 15 minutes). Brush loaf with remaining egg yolk mixture.

Bake in a 350° oven for 20 to 25 minutes or till golden and bread sounds hollow when tapped. Cool on a wire rack. Serve at room temperature. Store bread in the refrigerator. Makes 16 [20] servings.

One teaspoon yeast is recommended by our Test Kitchen for either loaf size (see page 6).

Nutrition information per serving: 113 calories, 4 g protein, 17 g carbohydrate, 3 g fat (1 g saturated), 27 mg cholesterol, 102 mg sodium, 71 mg potassium.

PEPPER AND PARMESAN BREAD

1 Pound	Ingredients	1½ Pound
¾ cup	water	1¼ cups
2½ cups	bread flour	3¼ cups
3 tablespoons	finely shredded Parmesan cheese	¼ cup
½ teaspoon	salt	¾ teaspoon
½ teaspoon	freshly ground black pepper	¾ teaspoon
⅛ teaspoon	garlic powder	⅛ teaspoon
1 teaspoon	active dry yeast *or* bread machine yeast	1 teaspoon
⅓ cup	finely shredded Parmesan cheese	½ cup
	Cornmeal	
1	slightly beaten egg white	1
1 tablespoon	water	1 tablespoon

Add the first 7 ingredients to the machine according to manufacturer's directions. Select dough cycle.

When cycle is complete, remove dough from machine. Cover and let rest 10 minutes. On a lightly floured surface, roll dough into a 15x10-inch rectangle. [Divide 1½ pound recipe in half and roll into two 10x8-inch rectangles.] Sprinkle the ⅓ cup [½ cup] Parmesan cheese atop the dough lengthwise down center of rectangle. Roll up jelly-roll style, starting from one of the long sides; seal well. Pinch and pull ends to taper.

Place seam side down on a greased baking sheet sprinkled with cornmeal. Combine egg white and water; brush over top of loaf. Cover and let rise till nearly double (about 45 minutes). With a very sharp knife, make 3 or 4 diagonal cuts about ¼ inch deep across the top of loaf.

Bake in a 375° oven for 35 to 40 minutes or till bread sounds hollow when tapped with your fingers. Remove from baking sheet; cool. Makes 16 [20] servings.

One teaspoon yeast is recommended by our Test Kitchen for either loaf size (see page 6).

Nutrition information per serving: 96 calories, 4 g protein, 16 g carbohydrate, 1 g fat (1 g saturated), 3 mg cholesterol, 131 mg sodium, 34 mg potassium.

SOUR CREAM-WHEAT DINNER ROLLS

1 Pound	Ingredients	1½ Pound
⅓ cup	milk	⅔ cup
⅓ cup	dairy sour cream	½ cup
1	egg	1
1 tablespoon	honey	2 tablespoons
1½ teaspoons	margarine *or* butter	2 teaspoons
1 cup	whole wheat flour	1½ cups
1 cup	bread flour	1½ cups
¼ cup	toasted wheat germ	⅓ cup
½ teaspoon	salt	¾ teaspoon
1 teaspoon	active dry yeast *or* bread machine yeast	1 teaspoon
	Margarine *or* butter, melted (optional)	

Add ingredients to machine (except melted margarine or butter) according to manufacturer's directions. Select dough cycle.

When cycle is complete, remove dough from machine. On a lightly floured surface, divide dough in half [thirds]. Let rest 10 minutes. Shape into Butterhorns, Rosettes, or Cloverleaf Rolls.

Butterhorns: Roll each half [third] of dough into an 8-inch circle. Brush each circle with about 1 tablespoon melted margarine or butter. Cut each circle into 8 wedges. Beginning at the wide ends, roll up dough wedges. With point sides down, place rolls 2 to 3 inches apart on greased baking sheets.

Rosettes: Divide each half [third] of dough into 8 pieces. Roll each piece into a 12-inch rope. Tie each rope in a loose knot, leaving 2 long ends. Tuck top end under roll. Bring bottom end up and tuck it into center of roll. Place rolls 2 to 3 inches apart on greased baking sheets.

Cloverleaf Rolls: Lightly grease 18 muffin cups [24 muffin cups]. Divide each half [third] of dough into 27 pieces [24 pieces]. Shape each piece into a ball, pulling edges under to make a smooth top. Place 3 balls, smooth side up, in each greased muffin cup.

Cover rolls and let rise in a warm place till nearly double (about 30 minutes). Bake in a 375° oven for 12 to 15 minutes or till golden brown. If desired, brush rolls with melted margarine or butter. Makes 16 or 18 [24] rolls.

One teaspoon yeast is recommended by our Test Kitchen for either size (see page 6).

Nutrition information per serving: 88 calories, 3 g protein, 14 g carbohydrate, 2 g fat (1g saturated), 16 mg cholesterol, 80 mg sodium, 79 mg potassium.

Bran-Bulgur Butterhorns

1 Pound	Ingredients	1½ Pound
1 cup	water	1 cup
¼ cup	bulgur wheat	⅓ cup
¾ cup	milk	1¼ cups
1½ teaspoons	shortening	2 teaspoons
2 cups	bread flour	3 cups
¼ cup	unprocessed wheat bran	⅓ cup
2 teaspoons	sugar	1 tablespoon
½ teaspoon	salt	¾ teaspoon
1 teaspoon	active dry yeast *or* bread machine yeast	1 teaspoon
2 tablespoons	margarine *or* butter, melted	3 tablespoons

In a small saucepan combine water and bulgur wheat. Bring to boiling; reduce heat. Cover and simmer for 5 minutes. Drain well; cool slightly.

Add cooked bulgur and remaining ingredients (except melted margarine or butter) to the machine according to manufacturer's directions. Select dough cycle.

When cycle is complete, remove dough from machine. On a lightly floured surface, divide dough in half [thirds]. Cover and let rest for 10 minutes.

Roll each half [third] of dough into an 8-inch circle. Brush each circle with about 1 *tablespoon* of the melted margarine or butter. Cut each circle into 8 wedges. Beginning at the wide ends, roll up dough wedges. Place rolls point sides down, 2 to 3 inches apart on greased baking sheets. Brush tops of rolls with melted margarine or butter.

Bake in a 400° oven for 12 to 15 minutes or till golden brown. Cool on a wire rack. Makes 16 [24] rolls.

One teaspoon yeast is recommended by our Test Kitchen for either size (see page 6).

Nutrition information per serving: 96 calories, 3 g protein, 16 g carbohydrate, 2 g fat (1 g saturated), 1 mg cholesterol, 90 mg sodium, 60 mg potassium.

CHEDDAR CHEESE BOWS

1 Pound	Ingredients	1½ Pound
⅔ cup	milk	1 cup
1	egg	1
2 cups	bread flour	3 cups
1 cup (4 ounces)	shredded cheddar, Swiss, or Monterey Jack cheese	1⅔ cups (6 ounces)
1 tablespoon	sugar	3 tablespoons
½ teaspoon	salt	¾ teaspoon
1 teaspoon	active dry yeast *or* bread machine yeast	1 teaspoon
	Milk	
¼ cup	finely shredded Parmesan cheese	⅓ cup

Add the first 7 ingredients to machine according to manufacturer's directions. Select dough cycle.

When cycle is complete, remove dough from machine. Cover and let rest 10 minutes. On a lightly floured surface, divide dough in half. Roll each half of the dough into a 12x8-inch rectangle [12-inch square]. Cut into eight [twelve] 12x1-inch strips.

On lightly greased or foil-lined baking sheets, shape each strip into a bow (form 2 loops and bring ends to center so they overlap about 1½ inches). Twist ends together once. Press dough together at center. Cover and let rise in a warm place till nearly double in size (20 to 30 minutes).

Brush rolls with additional milk; sprinkle with Parmesan cheese. Bake in a 375° oven for 12 minutes or till golden. Cool on wire racks. Makes 16 [24] rolls.

One teaspoon yeast is recommended by our Test Kitchen for either size (see page 6).

Nutrition information per serving: 104 calories, 5 g protein, 14 g carbohydrate, 3 g fat (2 g saturated), 21 mg cholesterol, 138 mg sodium, 49 mg potassium.

OATMEAL-CHERRY ROLLS

1 Pound	Ingredients	1½ Pound
¾ cup plus 2 tablespoons	milk	1¼ cups
1 tablespoon	margarine *or* butter	2 tablespoons
2 cups	bread flour	3 cups
⅓ cup	snipped, dried, tart, red cherries *or* raisins	½ cup
¼ cup	rolled oats	⅓ cup
¼ cup	unprocessed wheat bran	⅓ cup
2 teaspoons	brown sugar	1 tablespoon
½ teaspoon	salt	¾ teaspoon
1 teaspoon	active dry yeast *or* bread machine yeast	1 teaspoon
	Margarine *or* butter, melted, *or* milk	

Add ingredients to machine according to manufacturer's directions. Select dough cycle.

When cycle is complete, remove dough from machine. On a lightly floured surface, divide dough in half. Let rest 10 minutes. Divide each half of dough into 8 pieces [12 pieces]. Shape each piece of dough into a ball, pulling edges under to make a smooth top. Place rolls on lightly greased baking sheets. *or,* arrange 8 rolls [12 rolls] in each of 2 greased 9x1½-inch round baking pans. Cover and let rise till nearly double (about 30 minutes).

Bake in a 350° oven about 25 minutes or till golden brown. Brush rolls with melted margarine or butter or milk. Makes 16 [24] rolls.

One teaspoon yeast is recommended by our Test Kitchen for either size (see page 6).

Nutrition information per serving: 64 calories, 2 g protein, 11 g carbohydrate, 1 g fat (0 g saturated), 1 mg cholesterol, 58 mg sodium, 39 mg potassium.

WHOLE WHEAT ENGLISH MUFFINS

1 Pound	Ingredients	1½ Pound
¾ cup plus 2 tablespoons	milk	1¼ cups
1½ teaspoons	shortening	2 tablespoons
1⅓ cups	whole wheat flour	2 cups
⅔ cup	bread flour	1 cup
¼ cup	cracked wheat	⅓ cup
2 teaspoons	brown sugar	1 tablespoon
½ teaspoon	salt	¾ teaspoon
1 teaspoon	active dry yeast *or* bread machine yeast	1 teaspoon
	Cornmeal	

Add the first 8 ingredients to machine according to manufacturer's directions. Select dough cycle.

When cycle is complete, remove dough from machine. On a lightly floured surface, cover dough and let stand for 10 minutes. Roll dough to slightly less than ½ inch thick. Cut out muffins with a 4-inch-round biscuit cutter, rerolling scraps. Dip both sides of each muffin into cornmeal. (If necessary, to make cornmeal adhere, lightly brush muffins with water.) Cover and let rise in a warm place till very light (about 30 minutes). (*Or,* do not let rise. Cover and refrigerate for 2 to 24 hours.)

Cook muffins 4 or 5 at a time in an ungreased electric skillet at 325° for 25 to 30 minutes or till bread sounds hollow when tapped with your fingers, turning every 5 minutes. (Refrigerate any remaining muffins for up to 8 hours before cooking.) *Or,* cook over low heat on an ungreased large griddle or in several skillets for 25 to 30 minutes, turning frequently. Cool muffins thoroughly. To serve, split muffins horizontally and toast or broil. Makes 6 [8 or 9] muffins.

One teaspoon yeast is recommended by our Test Kitchen for either size (see page 6).

Nutrition information per serving: 214 calories, 8 g protein, 41 g carbohydrate, 3 g fat (1 g saturated), 3 mg cholesterol, 198 mg sodium, 219 mg potassium.

COFFEE AND CREAM ROLLS

1 Pound	Ingredients	1½ Pound
½ cup	milk	¾ cup
1	egg	1
3 tablespoons	margarine *or* butter	¼ cup
2 cups	bread flour	3 cups
2 tablespoons	sugar	3 tablespoons
½ teaspoon	salt	¾ teaspoon
1 teaspoon	active dry yeast *or* bread machine yeast	1 teaspoon
½ cup	coarsely chopped walnuts, toasted	¾ cup
1 tablespoon	margarine *or* butter, softened	2 tablespoons
3 tablespoons	packed brown sugar	⅓ cup
¼ cup	whipping cream	⅓ cup
¼ cup	Kahlua *or* coffee-flavored liqueur	⅓ cup

Add the first 7 ingredients to machine according to manufacturer's directions. Select dough cycle.

When cycle is complete, remove dough from machine. Cover and let rest 10 minutes. Meanwhile, sprinkle the walnuts in a greased 9x9x2-inch baking pan [2 greased 9x1½- or 8x1½-inch round baking pans].

For 1 pound recipe, on a lightly floured surface, roll the dough into a 12x8-inch rectangle. Spread with softened margarine. Sprinkle with brown sugar. Roll up jelly-roll style, starting from one of the long sides. Pinch seams to seal. Cut into 1-inch slices. Place rolls, cut sides down, in the prepared pan. Cover and let rise till nearly double (about 30 minutes).

[*For 1½ pound recipe,* divide dough in half. Roll half of the dough into a 9x8-inch rectangle. Spread with half of the softened margarine. Sprinkle with half of the brown sugar. Roll up jelly-roll style, starting from one of the long sides. Pinch seams to seal. Cut into 1-inch slices. Repeat with remaining dough, margarine, and brown sugar. Place rolls, cut sides down, in the prepared pans. Cover and let rise till nearly double (about 30 minutes).]

Combine the whipping cream and Kahlua. Pour [half of] the mixture over (each) pan of rolls. Bake in a 350° oven about 25 minutes or till browned. Cool slightly (5 minutes); invert onto serving plate. Serve warm. Makes 12 [18] rolls.

One teaspoon yeast is recommended by our Test Kitchen for either size (see page 6).

Nutrition information per serving: 209 calories, 5 g protein, 26 g carbohydrate, 9 g fat (2 g saturated), 22 mg cholesterol, 147 mg sodium, 92 mg potassium.

MAPLE-OAT BREAKFAST BUNS

1 Pound	Ingredients	1½ Pound
⅔ cup	milk	1 cup
1	egg	1
1 tablespoon	margarine *or* butter	2 tablespoons
2 cups	bread flour	3 cups
⅓ cup	oat flour*	⅔ cup
4 teaspoons	sugar	2 tablespoons
½ teaspoon	salt	¾ teaspoon
1 teaspoon	active dry yeast *or* bread machine yeast	1 teaspoon
⅓ cup	maple-flavored syrup	½ cup
¼ cup	packed brown sugar	⅓ cup
3 tablespoons	margarine *or* butter	¼ cup
¼ cup	chopped pecans *or* walnuts	⅓ cup
3 tablespoons	packed brown sugar	¼ cup
3 tablespoons	toasted rolled oats**	¼ cup
¼ teaspoon	ground cardamom	¼ teaspoon
1 tablespoon	margarine *or* butter, melted	2 tablespoons

Add the first 8 ingredients to machine according to manufacturer's directions. Select dough setting.

When cycle is complete, remove dough from machine. Cover and let rest for 10 minutes.

Meanwhile, in a small saucepan stir together the syrup, ¼ cup [⅓ cup] brown sugar, and 3 tablespoons [¼ cup] margarine or butter. Cook and stir over low heat till sugar is dissolved; do not boil. Spread mixture in the bottom of an ungreased 9x9x2-inch [13x9x2-inch] baking pan.

In a small mixing bowl stir together the chopped pecans or walnuts, 3 tablespoons [¼ cup] brown sugar, toasted rolled oats, and cardamom. Set aside.

For 1 pound recipe, on a lightly floured surface, roll dough into a 12x8-inch rectangle. Brush with 1 tablespoon melted margarine or butter. Sprinkle nut mixture over dough. Roll up jelly-roll style, starting from one of the long sides. Pinch seams to seal. Cut into 1-inch slices. Place rolls, cut sides down, in the prepared pan.

[*For 1½ pound recipe,* on a lightly floured surface, divide dough in half. Let rest 10 minutes. Roll half of the dough into a 9x8-inch rectangle. Brush 1 *tablespoon* of the melted margarine over dough. Sprinkle half of the nut mixture over the dough. Roll up jelly-roll style, starting from one of the long sides. Pinch seams to seal. Cut into 1-inch slices. Place rolls, cut sides down, in the prepared pan. Repeat with remaining dough and filling.]

Brush rolls with additional melted margarine or butter. Cover and let rise till nearly double (about 30 minutes). *or,* cover with waxed paper, then with clear plastic wrap. Refrigerate for 2 to 24 hours.

If chilled, let stand at room temperature, covered, about 20 minutes. Puncture any surface bubbles with a greased wooden toothpick. Bake in a 375° oven for 25 to 30 minutes or till golden brown. Cool slightly; invert onto a serving plate. Serve warm. Makes 12 [18] rolls.

One teaspoon yeast is recommended by our Test Kitchen for either size (see page 6).

*Note: For oat flour, place rolled oats in blender container. Blend on high speed about 1 minute or till oats become a fine powder.

**Note: For toasted rolled oats, place oats in a shallow baking pan. Bake in a 350° oven for 15 to 20 minutes or till oats are lightly browned; cool.

Nutrition information per serving: 184 calories, 5 g protein, 32 g carbohydrate, 4 g fat (1 g saturated), 19 mg cholesterol, 151 mg sodium, 85 mg potassium.

ALMOND LOAF

1 Pound	Ingredients	1½ Pound
½ cup	milk	-
1	egg	-
3 tablespoons	margarine *or* butter	-
2 cups	bread flour	-
3 tablespoons	sugar	-
½ teaspoon	salt	-
1 teaspoon	active dry yeast *or* bread machine yeast	-
½ of a 12½-ounce can (½ cup)	almond cake and pastry filling	-
¼ cup	miniature semisweet chocolate pieces	-
3 tablespoons	chopped toasted almonds	-

Add the first 7 ingredients to machine according to manufacturer's directions. Select dough cycle.

When cycle is complete, remove dough from machine. Let rest 10 minutes. On a lightly floured surface, roll dough into a 24x8-inch rectangle. In a small mixing bowl stir together the almond filling, 2 tablespoons of the chocolate pieces, and almonds. Spread filling over dough to ½ inch from edges.

Fold dough loosely from a short side, making about eight 3-inch-wide folds. (This is similar to rolling a jelly roll, except you fold the dough instead of rolling it.) Transfer to a baking sheet. Make 2½-inch-long cuts into the dough at ¾-inch intervals on one of the long sides. (Do not cut completely through to the other long side of dough roll.) Flip resulting ¾-inch pieces of dough to alternate sides (see cover photo). Twist each piece in the same direction, exposing the filling. Cover and let rise in a warm place till nearly double (about 30 minutes).

Bake in a 350° oven for 20 to 25 minutes or till golden. (If necessary, cover loosely with foil after 10 minutes to prevent overbrowning.) Sprinkle loaf with the remaining chocolate pieces while loaf is still warm. Serve warm. Makes 10 servings.

One teaspoon yeast is recommended by our Test Kitchen (see page 6).

Nutrition information per serving: 217 calories, 5 g protein, 36 g carbohydrate, 6 g fat (1 g saturated), 22 mg cholesterol, 182 mg sodium, 61 mg potassium.

SWIRLED CINNAMON-APPLE BREAD

1 Pound	Ingredients	1½ Pound
⅓ cup	milk	-
1	egg	-
2 tablespoons	margarine *or* butter	-
2 cups	bread flour	-
2 tablespoons	sugar	-
½ teaspoon	salt	-
1 teaspoon	active dry yeast *or* bread machine yeast	-
½ cup	shredded peeled apple	-
¾ cup	finely chopped, peeled apple	-
¼ cup	toasted chopped walnuts *or* pecans	-
¼ cup	packed brown sugar	-
1 teaspoon	ground cinnamon	-
1 tablespoon	margarine *or* butter	-
	Powdered sugar	-

Add the first 8 ingredients to machine according to manufacturer's directions. Select dough cycle.

When cycle is complete, remove dough from machine. Cover and let rest 10 minutes. Meanwhile, for filling, in a medium mixing bowl stir together the chopped apple, walnuts or pecans, brown sugar, and cinnamon. Set aside.

On a lightly floured surface, roll dough into a 14x9-inch rectangle. Spread with 1 tablespoon margarine or butter and filling. Beginning at both short ends, roll each end up, jelly-roll style, to center. Place loaf, rolled side up, in a greased 9x5x3-inch loaf pan. Cover and let rise till almost double (about 30 minutes).

Bake in a 350° oven for 30 minutes or till bread sounds hollow when top is tapped with your fingers. (If necessary, loosely cover with foil the last 10 minutes to prevent overbrowning.) Remove from pan; cool on a wire rack. Sprinkle with powdered sugar before serving. Makes 16 servings.

One teaspoon yeast is recommended by our Test Kitchen (see page 6).

Nutrition information per serving: 122 calories, 3 g protein, 20 g carbohydrate, 3 g fat (1 g saturated), 14 mg cholesterol, 91 mg sodium, 71 mg potassium.

APRICOT-AND-CHOCOLATE-FILLED LADDER LOAVES

1 Pound	Ingredients	1½ Pound
⅔ cup	milk	-
1	egg	-
1 tablespoon	margarine *or* butter	-
2 cups	bread flour	-
4 teaspoons	sugar	-
½ teaspoon	salt	-
1 teaspoon	active dry yeast *or* bread machine yeast	-
⅔ cup	dried apricots, snipped	-
½ cup	water	-
¼ cup	packed brown sugar	-
⅓ cup	semisweet chocolate pieces	-
½ cup	coconut	-
½ cup	sifted powdered sugar	-
¼ teaspoon	vanilla	-
2 to 3 teaspoons	milk	-

Add the first 7 ingredients to machine according to manufacturer's directions. Select dough cycle.

Meanwhile, for filling, in a small saucepan combine apricots and water. Bring to boiling; reduce heat. Simmer, uncovered, about 10 minutes or till water is nearly absorbed. *Do not drain.* Stir in brown sugar till dissolved. Stir in chocolate pieces till melted. Stir in coconut. Cool.

When cycle is complete, remove dough from machine. On a lightly floured surface, divide dough in half. Cover and let rest 10 minutes. Roll half of the dough into an 8-inch square. Place on a greased baking sheet. Spoon half of the filling in a 4-inch-wide strip down the center of dough, leaving 2 inches on each side. Slit dough at 1-inch intervals along each side of filling. Fold strips diagonally over filling, alternating from side to side. Repeat with remaining dough and filling. Cover and let rise in a warm place till double (about 45 minutes).

Bake in a 350° oven about 25 minutes or till golden. Transfer to a wire rack; cool. In a small bowl combine powdered sugar, vanilla, and enough milk to make an icing of drizzling consistency. Drizzle over loaves. If desired, freeze loaves, un-iced, for up to 3 months. Makes 2 loaves, 8 servings each.

One teaspoon yeast is recommended by our Test Kitchen (see page 6).

Nutrition information per serving: 144 calories, 3 g protein, 25 g carbohydrate, 4 g fat (1 g saturated), 14 mg cholesterol, 87 mg sodium, 154 mg potassium.

SPICED CHOCOLATE AND RYE COFFEE CAKE

1 Pound	Ingredients	1½ Pound
⅔ cup	milk	-
¼ cup	miniature semisweet chocolate pieces, melted and cooled	-
1	egg	-
3 tablespoons	margarine *or* butter	-
1¾ cups	bread flour	-
½ cup	rye flour	-
2 tablespoons	brown sugar	-
½ teaspoon	salt	-
1 teaspoon	active dry yeast *or* bread machine yeast	-
¼ cup	miniature semisweet chocolate pieces	-
2 tablespoons	sugar	-
¼ teaspoon	ground cinnamon	-
1 tablespoon	margarine *or* butter, softened	-
½ cup	sifted powdered sugar	-
1 to 2 teaspoons	milk	-

Add the first 9 ingredients to machine according to manufacturer's directions, adding the ¼ cup melted chocolate pieces with the milk. Select dough cycle.

Meanwhile, in a small mixing bowl stir together the remaining ¼ cup chocolate pieces, the sugar, and cinnamon. Set aside.

When cycle is complete, remove dough from machine. Cover and let rest 10 minutes. On a lightly floured surface, roll dough into an 18x8-inch rectangle. Spread 1 tablespoon softened margarine or butter over dough. Sprinkle with chocolate-sugar-cinnamon mixture. Roll up jelly-roll style, starting from one of the long sides. Pinch seams to seal. Place on a greased baking sheet, curving the loaf into a crescent or horseshoe shape. Cover and let rise till nearly double (1 to 1¼ hours).

Bake in a 350° oven about 30 minutes or till coffee cake sounds hollow when tapped with your fingers. (If necessary, cover with foil the last 10 minutes to prevent overbrowning.) Cool on a wire rack.

Before serving, in a small mixing bowl stir together the powdered sugar and enough milk to make an icing of drizzling consistency. Drizzle over cooled coffee cake. Makes 16 servings.

One teaspoon yeast is recommended by our Test Kitchen (see page 6).

Nutrition information per serving: 151 calories, 3 g protein, 24 g carbohydrate, 5 g fat (1 g saturated), 14 mg cholesterol, 110 mg sodium, 71 mg potassium.

APRICOT-ALMOND WREATH

1 Pound	Ingredients	1½ Pound
⅓ cup	buttermilk	-
⅓ cup	orange juice	-
1	egg	-
2 tablespoons	margarine *or* butter	-
2¼ cups	bread flour	-
2 tablespoons	sugar	-
½ teaspoon	salt	-
½ teaspoon	ground cardamom	-
⅛ teaspoon	ground nutmeg	-
1 teaspoon	active dry yeast *or* bread machine yeast	-
½ cup	snipped dried apicots	-
¼ cup	toasted chopped almonds	-
	Milk	
	Orange Glaze (optional)	
	Snipped dried apricots (optional)	

Add the first 12 ingredients to machine according to manufacturer's directions.

When cycle is complete, remove dough from machine. On a lightly floured surface, divide dough in half. Cover and let rest 10 minutes. Roll each half into an evenly thick rope 24 inches long. Lay the 2 ropes side by side and 1 inch apart; twist together loosely. Join ends to form a circle. Place on a lightly greased baking sheet. Cover and let rise till nearly double (about 45 minutes). Brush dough with milk. Bake in a 375° oven for 20 to 25 minutes or till golden. Cool on a wire rack. Makes 12 servings.

One teaspoon yeast is recommended by our Test Kitchen (see page 6).

Orange Glaze: In a small mixing bowl stir together ½ cup sifted *powdered sugar* and 1/2 teaspoon *vanilla*. Stir in enough *orange juice* (2 to 3 teaspoons) to make a glaze of drizzling consistency. Drizzle over top of wreath. If desired, arrange additional snipped dried apricots atop wreath in glaze.

Nutrition information per serving: 159 calories, 5 g protein, 26 g carbohydrate, 4 g fat (1 g saturated), 18 mg cholesterol, 126 mg sodium, 159 mg potassium.

MINCEMEAT COFFEE BREAD

1 Pound	Ingredients	1½ Pound
⅓ cup	milk	-
⅓ cup	prepared mincemeat	-
1	egg	-
2 tablespoons	margarine *or* butter	-
2¼ cups	bread flour	-
½ teaspoon	salt	-
1 teaspoon	active dry yeast *or* bread machine yeast	-
½ cup	prepared mincemeat	-
½ cup	sifted powdered sugar	-
¼ teaspoon	vanilla	-
2 to 3 teaspoons	milk	-

Add the first 7 ingredients to machine according to manufacturer's directions. Select dough cycle.

When cycle is complete, remove dough from machine. Cover and let rest 10 minutes. Divide dough in half. Roll half into a 9-inch circle. Place in a greased 9x1½-inch round baking pan. Spread the remaining mincemeat over the top of the dough in the pan to within 1 inch of edge. Roll remaining half of dough into a 10-inch circle. Place on top of mincemeat. Cut top dough into 16 wedges, cutting to about 1 inch from center of dough. Twist each strip twice. Tuck each strip end under bottom dough. Cover and let rise till nearly double (about 30 minutes).

Bake in a 375° oven for 25 minutes or till top sounds hollow when tapped with your fingers. Cover with foil during the last 10 minutes of baking to prevent overbrowning. Invert onto a plate; turn over and cool on wire rack.

Meanwhile, for glaze, in a small mixing bowl stir together the powdered sugar and vanilla. Add enough milk to make a glaze of drizzling consistency. Drizzle over bread. Serve warm or cool. Makes 12 servings.

One teaspoon yeast is recommended by our Test Kitchen (see page 6).

Nutrition information per serving: 178 calories, 4 g protein, 33 g carbohydrate, 3 g fat (1 g saturated), 18 mg cholesterol, 179 mg sodium, 87 mg potassium.

CHERRY-ALMOND COFFEE BREAD

1 Pound	Ingredients	1½ Pound
⅔ cup	milk	-
1	egg	-
3 tablespoons	margarine *or* butter	-
2¼ cups	bread flour	-
2 tablespoons	sugar	-
½ teaspoon	salt	-
1 teaspoon	active dry yeast *or* bread machine yeast	-
⅓ cup	cherry *or* seedless red raspberry preserves	-
3 tablespoons	toasted sliced almonds	-
2 tablespoons	margarine *or* butter, softened	-
½ cup	sifted powdered sugar	-
1½ teaspoons	margarine *or* butter, softened	-
¼ teaspoon	vanilla	-
1 to 2 teaspoons	milk	-

Add the first 7 ingredients to machine according to manufacturer's directions.

When cycle is complete, remove dough from machine. Cover and let rest 10 minutes. On a lightly floured surface, roll dough into a 16x8-inch rectangle.

Combine preserves, 2 *tablespoons* of the sliced almonds, and 2 tablespoons margarine or butter. Spread over dough. Roll up jelly-roll style, starting from one of the long sides. Pinch seams to seal. Using a sharp knife, cut the roll of dough in half lengthwise. Beginning in the center of a greased 9x1½-inch round baking pan, loosely coil one strip of dough, cut side up. Loosely coil second strip of dough around first strip. Cover and let rise in a warm place till double (20 to 30 minutes).

Bake in a 350° oven about 35 minutes or till bread sounds hollow when lightly tapped with your fingers. (If necessary, cover loosely with foil the last 10 to 15 minutes to prevent overbrowning.) Remove from pan. Cool on a wire rack.

Meanwhile, for glaze, in a small mixing bowl stir together the powdered sugar, 1½ teaspoons margarine or butter, and vanilla. Stir in enough milk to make a glaze of drizzling consistency. Drizzle over bread; sprinkle bread with remaining sliced almonds. Makes 16 servings.

One teaspoon yeast is recommended by our Test Kitchen (see page 6).

Nutrition information per serving: 160 calories, 3 g protein, 24 g carbohydrate, 6 g fat (1 g saturated), 14 mg cholesterol, 123 mg sodium, 63 mg potassium.

PEANUT BUTTER-CHOCOLATE BUBBLE RING

1 Pound	Ingredients	1½ Pound
⅔ cup	milk	-
¼ cup	creamy peanut butter	-
1	egg	-
2 cups	bread flour	-
4 teaspoons	sugar	-
½ teaspoon	salt	-
1 teaspoon	active dry yeast *or* bread machine yeast	-
20	milk-chocolate kisses	-
½ cup	sugar	-
½ teaspoon	ground cinnamon	-
¼ cup	margarine *or* butter, melted	-

Add the first 7 ingredients to machine according to manufacturer's directions. Select dough cycle.

When cycle is complete, remove dough from machine. Cover and let rest 10 minutes. On a lightly floured surface, divide dough into 20 pieces. Using your hands, flatten each piece of dough into a 3-inch circle. Place an unwrapped chocolate kiss in the center of each round of dough. Bring the edge of the dough up and around the chocolate kiss to form a ball. Pinch the edges of the dough together to seal firmly.

In a small mixing bowl stir together the ½ cup sugar and cinnamon. Dip each ball of dough into the melted margarine or butter, then roll it in the sugar-cinnamon mixture. Arrange half of the coated balls of dough in the bottom of a greased 6½-cup oven-proof ring mold. Make a second layer, positioning the balls of dough for the second layer between the balls of dough in the first layer. (Do not let bread rise.)

Bake in a 375° oven about 20 minutes or till golden brown. Cool 1 minute on a wire rack. Invert onto a serving plate; remove ring mold. Serve coffee cake warm. Makes 10 servings.

One teaspoon yeast is recommended by our Test Kitchen (see page 6).

Nutrition information per serving: 286 calories, 7 g protein, 40 g carbohydrate, 12 g fat (2 g saturated), 24 mg cholesterol, 215 mg sodium, 147 mg potassium.